Praise for the Author

Karon writes powerfully of her own experiences of grief. Her words are raw, honest and potent and her expertise and compassion shine through. We can all relate to her journey as she balances grief and acceptance through writing that cuts through, alternating hard, sharp words with beautifully crafted sentences that hold the promise of healing. Her writing is a great accompaniment to her other work in the ongoing journey to make bereavement and grief a little easier.

Alison Hill
Author and Editor

Having had the privilege to participate in Karon's grief timeline and healing workshop, I wholeheartedly recommend Karon and her work to anyone who has experienced any loss in their life. I have experienced many approaches to grief and loss and healing and timeline work yet Karon's approach took me beyond my expectations. With Karon's heartfelt guidance and love I made connections that I had never before and was able to embody and release the insights and healing. A truly profound experience that I recommend with all my heart and soul.

Debra Coulson

I went to Karon's workshop with a very open mind and not sure really what to expect. What I did get was a far more than I could have imagined. The gently guided processes gave me space to be vulnerable while being in a very loving, caring, safe environment. This allowed me to get some insightful informative information that will really help me on my journey of healing. Thank you so much Karon

Victoria Howard-McRae

The Grief Journey

Global Publishing Group
Australia • New Zealand • Singapore • America • London

The Grief Journey

Inspirational Stories & Strategies to Move & Motivate You To Successful Healing

RETT KAKOSCHKE   JULIUS CZERNY   KAREN SYDNÈ-SCOTT   LOUIS REED   JAMES THOMAS

PETREA KING   SENATOR KRISTINA KENEALLY   SUSAN TEMPLEMAN MP   GREG ALEXANDER

Karon Coombs

First Edition 2020

National Library of Australia
Cataloguing-in-Publication entry:

The Grief Journey: Inspirational Stories & Strategies to Move & Motivate You To Successful Healing - Karon Coombs

1st ed.
ISBN: 978-1-925288-92-6 (pbk.)

A catalogue record for this book is available from the National Library of Australia

Published by Global Publishing Group
PO Box 517 Mt Evelyn, Victoria 3796 Australia
Email Info@GlobalPublishingGroup.com.au

For further information about orders:
Phone: +61 3 9726 4133

I dedicate this book to anyone who has ever dared to open themselves to the profound depths of grief. It takes enormous courage, faith, strength and vulnerability to experience the complex emotions of intense pining, rage, guilt, jealousy, sorrow, despair, shame and helplessness to complete the healing that the grief journey offers. It is a complex and chaotic journey that can leave you reeling and confused. As you come out of the depths it can also offer gifts for an improved and meaningful life. I send you healing loving energy as you walk your individual path and may you find your gifts in loss.

Karon Coombs

Acknowledgements

Writing this book has been such an awesome experience and involved much support from so many incredible people to bring it to life.

My deepest gratitude to all the amazing people who gave me the opportunity to interview them and hear the intimate details of their losses and bereavement as they shared their grief journey. Each opened their hearts and allowed their vulnerability to shine through, so that we may all take their hard-won wisdom and apply it to our grief from the many losses life hands each of us. They each shared some tears as they revealed their stories which are raw, incisive, inspiring and fascinating. It has been an honour and a tremendous privilege to learn from every one of you. I'm sure thousands of people's lives will be positively influenced by the deeply personal stories and insights that you have shared.

Thelma Lyell, my great friend and clever editor who gave so generously of her time, wisdom and love. You have been instrumental in making this a book the reader just can't put down.

To my wonderful husband, Bill Coombs, who is unflinching in supporting me on my wild and wonderful ideas and without whose love this book simply would not have been completed. I love you dearly Bill and I am grateful every day for our time as soulmates in this lifetime. You have contributed so much!

To the three who changed my world, my children; Ben who taught me to be fearless, and Jordy who taught me to savour the sweet moments in life. Thank you for continually bringing so much love and joy into my life. And Dashiell who died, teaching me all about the depth of love and grief. I love you all dearly from the bottom of my heart.

To the other special children in my life, Denning and Katrina, Penny, Rebecca, and my gorgeous granddaughter Poppy. You all bring a loving dimension to our family as you shine bright just being yourself.

Heather Gwilliam OAM CF, for giving me your insights into the many aspects of coordination of an evacuation centre following a bushfire/disaster, and for your ongoing love, friendship and support. Your love and light shines brightly in this world when people need it most.

To my mentor, Lou Reed who has encouraged me every step of the way, I am so grateful our paths crossed. I have grown so much under your loving spiritual guidance.

A big thank you to my publisher, Global Publishing Group, and in particular Darren Stephens and Jackie Tallentyre. The writing journey has many ups and downs and these people have been there for me as I struggled and as I rejoiced in my successes, always offering wise advice, encouragement and sharing in my joy.

To my dear friends who have accepted I needed to focus for a year on this project to bring it to fruition and have accepted me not being so freely available as a friend. They are true friends who know good friends are like stars, you don't have to see them to know they are there. I am so grateful to have you in my life and always send you loving energy.

66

Grieving is a journey to your core where you find yourself, discovering strength, resilience and the true depth of love.

Karon Coombs

FREE BONUS GIFT
Valued at $195 – but yours <u>free!</u>

There are **SPECIAL RECORDED INTERVIEWS** with expert author Karon Coombs as well as other people's **POWERFUL STORIES** plus discounts for numerous services

✔ Top tips to improve your grief journey.

✔ What to say to a grieving person.

✔ How to be a great friend to someone bereaved.

✔ How to improve your communication with a grieving person.

Claim your FREE BONUS GIFT NOW by going to www.TheGriefJourney.com.au/Book-Bonus for instant access.

Table Of Contents

> ❝
>
> *As I limped through each day with my aching emptiness, I found that society is not geared to listening to people in grief. But it is in sharing our story and having it witnessed that we find healing.*
>
> Karon Coombs

Introduction

When we cease to resist our grief, we learn that painful as it may be, grief is an integral part of elder wisdom, a force that humbles and deepens our hearts, connects us to the grief of the world, and enables us to be of help.

Ram Dass

Each chapter in this book reveals a fascinating and awe-inspiring story of the grief journey of people I interviewed. There is a Member of Parliament, a Senator, famous footballer, famous healer, famous lifesaver, online entrepreneur, builder/spiritual healer, survivor of the Christchurch Earthquakes and the founder of a wonderful organisation that provides support for children grieving the loss of a parent/carer. It is a deep dive into the psychology of grief. You will learn the many ways people cope with loss and grief. There is great advice if you are searching for ways to manage the pain of your own grief and to find meaning in your loss. You will find things you could do to better support a friend or family member who is grieving. Some chapters will bring tears, but you will also understand that there is healing to be found in expressing your painful story. This is a book that offers hope knowing that others have been able to move through their grief to lead fulfilling, happy and successful lives. As you read, you will discover there is a theme that connects the stories; creating a legacy has benefits not only for yourself but also for others in the world. Each person has taken their experience and created something beneficial for others and found healing for themselves in doing so.

I grew up hearing there are two things you can be sure of in life. Death and taxes. Loss should have been included. We have no choice when it comes to loss. Eventually loss visits every one of us. It often begins in childhood with the death of our dearly loved pets and grandparents. It could be a move to a new home and new school, or the breakup of our parent's marriage and the accompanying loss of regular contact with one parent. James Thomas's chapter gives us information on how to support children who lose a parent or sibling to death. His principles however, can be used in other examples of childhood loss, so adults become better at supporting children in grief and resource them with tools and resilience. Imagine the resilience born of teaching a child to cope with loss and how that will prepare them for the losses we know they will experience throughout their lives.

You will learn strategies, both healthy and not so healthy, to help you determine what you will use. There are stories of courage and bravery beyond belief, stories to warm your heart and stories that will bring tears to your eyes. Narratives so breathtaking they will be embedded in your heart and soul for years to come. As Petrea King says, "So much has been written about the process of grief, but I think actually hearing the words of other people who have grieved is really powerful. Because oftentimes people articulate exactly what you felt even before you found the words for it yourself and it speeds up your own process of self-understanding."

Our society acknowledges there is grief following the death of someone we love. However, as a society we do not really acknowledge the many other types of losses we experience, e.g. marriage breakdown leading to divorce, the loss of health, fertility, work and career, home, culture, self-esteem and the grief associated with these losses. This book explores some of these.

I was motivated to write this book because I have always been fascinated by people's stories. Also, my professional career as an oncology/palliative care nurse consultant for over 20 years, necessarily led me to become an expert on death, loss and grief. I was fortunate to attend an Elisabeth Kübler-Ross retreat, learning from the world expert at the time how to improve my care of people with a life-threatening disease, and their families. I lost count of how many seminars and workshops by Mal McKissock (Australian bereavement expert) I attended. I thought I knew what I was doing and what the patients and carers experience of grief was like. I was receiving good feedback from families on my work.

And then my son Dashiell died. It blindsided me.

That's when my personal understanding of grief took me to places in my heart where no one should have to go. Deep black holes that threatened to swallow me up. Places that made death seem alluring. I was catapulted there after my third son, my baby, unexpectedly died. It changed everything about my life.

After the funeral, I was flung into a deep black pit of despair. Forced to confront the most intense feelings of rage, guilt, jealousy, sorrow and helplessness. I was left exhausted, battered and vulnerable. Devastated beyond belief.

The world became a dangerous place. On a simple trip to the shops, a glimpse of a baby, taunting me with its life, would send me spinning down into that pit again. The long and arduous climb out could take hours or days. I no longer felt certain about my future, I no longer felt certain about who I was. My grief journey was a thousand times worse than my worst imagining. My two other sons lost their mother for a while, but in their need for care, I found a reason to live.

Our society envies and celebrates success, money, material possessions. To reach out in caring is not highly valued. Yet it is the essential foundation of any society. It is essential to our spiritual growth, to the very essence of each one of us, both in the giving and receiving.

The people who have listened to my pain with their hearts, who didn't run away from my tears, are friends I shall treasure for ever. I needed them to help me find the courage to face my grief, to allow the pain to wash through me. Deal with each issue as it arose. To allow the healing of my tattered soul.

I knew that if I could face my grief, I would open myself, not only to feelings of desolation and despair, but also to strengths and a new richness would be woven into the threads of my life.

I eventually found the determination and fortitude to take my pain and turn it into Dashiell's and my legacy for the world. I created an award-winning documentary about parents who had lost a baby, called *A Part of You Dies*. I used it to educate healthcare professionals about providing better care for bereaved parents, to improve their outcome.

Over the following eight years I delivered workshops based on the documentary to midwives, social workers and doctors. I wanted to make a difference for future parents and I desperately needed to create meaning for my son's death. The documentary was subsequently bought by a distributor in the Netherlands. I am proud that I created systemic change that continues to have a ripple effect today.

I have since spoken at an international conference and many State/ National Conferences on grief and bereavement. I also taught Loss and Grief Counselling at the Australian College of Applied Psychology, universities and hospitals. My extensive knowledge in this area is both professional and personal. That puts me in a unique position to have a deep understanding of the chaotic and unpredictable grief journey and the value in doing grief work to support your recovery.

Reading you will discover there are gifts in loss for all of us, but it is hard to find them in the midst of despair. Gifts such as a new appreciation of life, new possibilities, improved relationships with others, personal strength and spiritual changes. Kristina Keneally said of her daughter, Caroline, "She enlarged my understanding of love and loss, and she taught me to survive. She made me brave, almost fearless."

Loss can lift the lid off life and shake your beliefs to the core. It is a journey into self as we discover our essential nature, our strengths and courage, the hero within us all and new beliefs about the world. Finding meaning in loss can give you a new perspective, new purpose and reignite your passion for life.

I have distilled the essence of each interview at the conclusion of each chapter. As you read, I expect you will feel inspired and moved to a better understanding of your grief work. I hope you will be able to move forward and lead a happy and fulfilling life with meaning while honouring the memory of the person or thing you have lost. The book is full of easy and practical advice that will guarantee your road to successful recovery.

Karon Coombs

Chapter 1

Petrea King

"There is within each one of us a potential for goodness beyond our imagining; for giving which seeks no reward; listening without judgement; for loving unconditionally."

Elisabeth Kübler-Ross

PETREA KING Biography

Founder and CEO

Quest for Life Foundation

Petrea King is CEO of the Quest for Life Foundation which she established in 1989 after a series of personal traumas. She is a naturopath, yoga and meditation teacher. She opened the Quest for Life Centre in Bundanoon, NSW, in 1998. It is in this residential centre that Petrea and a team of facilitators, psychotherapists, yoga and meditation teachers, psychologists and other health professionals conduct 30 five-day programs each year for people experiencing physical, emotional or mental trauma including post-traumatic stress injuries. Quest facilitators conduct a further hundred one or two-day workshops in rural, regional and remote Australia each year.

She is a best-selling author of nine books and a dozen meditation practices, is a frequent keynote speaker at medical and other conferences, a facilitator, teacher and trainer and, for the past twenty years, has been a monthly guest on the ABC's *Midweek Conference* and *Nightlife* where she discusses the challenges of living a meaningful life in the midst of illness, trauma, difficult circumstances and tragedy.

Quest for Life programs, support and meditation groups, and workshops have helped more than 120,000 people living with physical and mental health issues. These programs provide participants with a proven, effective and holistic approach to creating physical, mental, emotional health and wellbeing.

Petrea has received the Advance Australia Award, Citizen of the Year and the Centenary Medal for her contribution to the community. She has been nominated for Australian of the Year each year since 2003 as well as being an NSW finalist for Senior Australian of the Year in 2011. In 2003 she was celebrated on Channel 9's *This Is Your Life* and has been featured twice on *Australian Story*, *Compass* and many other television and radio productions.

Quest for Life
FOUNDATION

The Interview

Petrea: Karon I think we met in the 80s, over 30 years ago.

Karon: You were starting to facilitate groups in your lounge room. I was a palliative care nurse visiting people in their homes. You went from that lounge room to this beautiful property of Quest for Life.

Petrea: I know. Oh well, without a dream, nothing happens. Wendie, my partner thought I was nuts as the Quest for Life Foundation didn't have any funds to purchase this property. The Chair of the Board and everybody else was saying, "Yes, that's nice, Petrea – but we don't have the funds." I said, "I don't know how it's going to happen, but I'm sure it's meant for us."

Karon: Before you were successful, could you have imagined you would end up here?

Petrea: There's no way I would have imagined I would have ended up here when I was in my 30s, and when I was very sick, because I had such low self-esteem. I knew I was on the earth for something. I'd hitched my wagon to Swami Kriyananda because he did wonderful work and he was a brilliant and creative man and founded the Ananda Community. But it wasn't my path. It was a good path. Now I feel like I've arrived exactly where I needed to be and everything that happened in my life has brought me to being where I am now.

Karon: Do you think there were things that happened in your childhood that were directing you in this?

Petrea: Definitely, I always had a lot of compassion. I found animals suffering really hard to cope with as well as human suffering. I think when I was eight; I was holding a man's head after a car accident, until the ambulance arrived because he was fitting due to a brain haemorrhage. I always had that innate desire to be of some sort of service to other people or animals. I started the World Wildlife Fund in Australia when I was twelve years old. When I was admitted into hospital, I had to give it up because I had so many surgeries on my legs and I couldn't manage the responsibilities of the World Wildlife Fund.

Karon: Amazing! In your writings you talk about life being quite stressful in the 18 months leading up to your diagnosis of leukemia.

Petrea: My brother Brenden was always a very complex person. He told me before we were both ten, that he knew he had to kill himself by the time he was thirty. I reasoned that was my life's purpose; I'm here to keep Brenden safe. I remember thinking at that time, I have to grow up really quickly so I can look after Brenden. In the next 15 months I grew 23 centimetres. That is what deranged the bone growth in my legs and my knees swivelled in and started dislocating. At age 13, I left school and went into hospital and virtually had three months in, one month out, three months in, one month out, nine months in, one month out for three years. This worked well for me because I was away from Brenden who I adored, but also found very scary. I wasn't able to go to school but I wasn't interested in what they were teaching in school. I was much more interested in nature and the purpose of human existence. Deeper life questions, none of which were addressed by anyone I knew.

Brenden did attempt suicide several times. Each time we saved him. He finally took his life in Kathmandu at the age of 32. When he was 30, he'd found meditation and completely cleaned up his life. He was very happy. We all went into that sense of, "Oh, thank heavens, Brenden's okay." When the phone call came from Kathmandu, it was a huge shock to us all because we really thought he was over his mental distress. There was no body, no funeral, no memorial, no packing up of possessions. It was very challenging really to come to terms with the reality of his death when there were no motions to go through. To this day, I can see a head in the crowd or a posture and think, "Oh, I wonder if that's Brenden?" even though intellectually, I know that's nonsense. If you don't see the body and there is no ritual, funeral, memorial or distribution of possessions, then it is hard to take on the reality of a person's death. I think the heart always looks for people we've loved and lost and wonders how they might be now. They're frozen in time and he'll always be 32 years old to me.

After Brenden's death, my husband and I moved to America to do our yoga and meditation teacher training. We'd only been there four weeks when I thought he'd gone for a long walk, but he'd returned to Australia; leaving me penniless, with two small children in this meditation community, living in a geodesic dome. The children's distress was considerable which included night terrors and separation anxiety. It was after that, that I was diagnosed with acute myeloid leukemia and was given three months to live. I was told I wouldn't see Christmas. My very first reaction was relief, because I was still feeling grief-stricken and responsible for not having been able to stop Brenden from ending his life. Ever since he'd told me of his plan, I had felt like he is my responsibility – and I'd failed him and my family, as I had not kept him safe.

Karon: You grew up with those beliefs. They are so hard to let go of.

Petrea: Absolutely. They become second nature to you. It's often grief and suffering that drive us towards peace and healing, so desperate becomes our need for relief from our despair.

Karon: You didn't have an easy life, did you?

Petrea: Well no, but life isn't a competition to see who's suffering the most. **Whatever our suffering, it's our suffering, and we must learn to find a pathway through, otherwise we can become consumed, embittered, resentful or dispirited.** Grief ripped the lid off all the previous traumas I'd experienced. There'd been the years in hospital and chronic pain; I was raped not long after leaving hospital the last time. I was at a church fellowship meeting in someone's home, lying down in one of the bedrooms due to pain when this man I knew vaguely came into the room and raped me. I had no voice to call for help. I'd gone into nursing and had injured my back. After that, I moved to the Netherlands where my brothers were both living. I took a lot of LSD and my anxiety and depression deepened. Brenden's despair was palpable, and I felt so much anxiety around him. I went into relationships with people who were either violent or emotionally abusive, if nothing else, and the chronic pain, was very wearing. There was domestic violence in my marriage. I had two gorgeous kids who were my joy. I was definitely not at peace in myself. Like many people, I lived with a highly polished façade that I hoped would fool anyone and distract them from any deeper enquiry into my world. It wasn't until I had leukemia, and was facing my mortality, that my own peace of mind became an imperative to address. I fully expected to die, but I wanted to find peace before I died. For me, that meant weeping tears, loads of tears, buckets of tears.

Karon: Was all your grief from all those incidents coming to the surface?

Petrea: Yes, because I'd never cried up until then. In our family, we coped. No matter what traumatic things happened, we put on a stiff upper lip. However, it's not easy to kiss someone who's keeping a stiff upper lip! A stiff upper lip can keep everyone at arm's length! The combination of illness, profound grief and physical exhaustion led me into that deep place of despair. Up swelled all the grief, the losses, all the shame, the emotional distress from the past which I could no longer keep submerged. It was a very cathartic period. **I was terrified of crying because I thought if I start, I might never stop or I'll disintegrate into a million fragments, and that'll be the end of me.**

Karon: Which are common feelings for grieving people.

Petrea: Exactly. I don't think as a culture we're terribly good at making space for grief. Australians tend to give each other three months and then you're somehow expected to be over it. Anyone who has grieved knows that you don't grieve for three months or six months or a year, you grieve for a lifetime. Hopefully, in time you become more comfortable with your own inner landscape of grief and more familiar with the territory, more familiar with the things that tip you into that territory. **Grief can spring out of drawers, come to you on a perfume or a snatch of music, and your right back at day one again.**

Karon: It's so good to hear you say that. People get sick of being told 'it's time to move on', it's healthier if it becomes a part of who you are. The changed person you are after experiencing the loss.

Petrea: Exactly. I think we're often uncomfortable around emotional expression and people can be very unsympathetic. People's names drift out of conversation as if that person never existed. It's hard, as the years pass, to even find people who knew your loved one. Grief is such a solitary experience. Family members often grieve in very different ways.

Someone will want to talk about the person who's died. Another doesn't want to hear anything. **Some will fill up their life with busyness so they don't have to 'go there'. Other people will get stuck in grief. We need to make space for grief, otherwise it comes out in messy ways and that's less helpful.**

Karon: We don't realise that our behaviours are actually the grief coming out.

Petrea: That's right.

Karon: Do you think those really, stressful life events actually led to your diagnosis of leukemia?

Petrea: I think it's always a challenge to know why anyone develops a life-threatening illness. I did have hundreds of x-rays during those three years in hospital as a 13, 14, 15-year-old. I was bedbound for many months and my femur wouldn't unite after one of the osteotomies where they'd cut my femur and turned my lower leg out 11 degrees. My leg was in traction for nine months. I sometimes had two x-rays a week to see if there was any progress in the union of the bone. Portable x-ray machines were relatively new in the 60s and hospital staff didn't always remember to bring the heavy protective blanket meant to put over you to stop radiation. I think maybe I received more radiation than was healthy.

Sometimes I think when there is grief, or it can be a pregnancy, or it can be another very stressful event, our immune system dips. We know pregnancy can put a strain on the body. We know that stress can put a strain on the body. My immune system was probably suppressed when I was going through the strain of grief and then the loss of my marriage. There's no medical proof of that as a causation though. More oncologists believe that stress and grief, in particular, can lower one's immune system so that if there is a possibility for cancer, it can activate then.

Karon: That's really interesting. You were left alone with two children and a diagnosis that you wouldn't live past three months. How did that impact on your children?

Petrea: Well, I was trying to protect them as much as I could from the loss they were experiencing. My mother flew to America and brought us home. My children had to go and live with their father because I became very sick. Handing my children over to my former husband didn't give me any joy because he was violent with me and I knew he would take things out on my daughter, Kate. At the age of seven she came and sat on my bed one day and said, "Mum, you're sick. If you need to meditate to get well, I think you should go back to America." I hadn't even told the children I was sick, because I didn't want everyone looking at me with coffin eyes, as if I was dead already. I wouldn't let anyone even say the word leukemia.

Karon: Amazing wisdom from a seven-year-old.

Petrea: It came as such a shock because my mother had brought me home to die. The only treatment for my type of leukemia, was an experimental treatment in the USA. While the treatment would probably extend my life by a few weeks, it was very expensive, would make me very ill and only available in America. I decided against having the treatment because I felt like I'd rather die, me and leukemia, rather than having the confusion of, am I sick from the treatment, am I sick from leukemia? There was a part of me that was a bit over life at that point as well – because of chronic pain, past traumas and grief and all that had happened. After a lot of discussion with my family, I returned to my dear friends in America. That led me to Italy because Swami Kriyananda was about to lecture there, and he thought I should go with him.

It's a much longer story but I finally ended up in the beautiful little town of Assisi. However, I couldn't cope with the noise and busyness of Assisi and I craved quiet and a space to reflect and rest. One day, I stumbled upon a monastery about four-and-a-half kilometres up the mountain, the Eremo delle Carceri – the Monastery of the 'Cells' or 'Caves'. St Francis and his close followers used to retreat to these caves within Mount Subasio. The monastery built around these caves is very peaceful. When I entered St Francis' cave, I felt like I'd found the right place to reflect and meditate and thought, "I'll either die in here or I'll find peace, but I'm not leaving". That's when the tears started. I couldn't keep them at bay any longer. The Superiore of the Monastery, Padre

Llarino, was very worried that he had this pale, divorced Anglican holed up in his little Catholic cave and that if I died in there, it would be very bad for business! He insisted that I eat. The first night he came and dragged me upstairs and sat me at an ancient table that monks had been eating off for centuries and he put a meal in front of me. The meal contained meat. I'd been a very strict vegetarian for 15 years. There was a chunk of white bread and, as a naturopath, I'd been telling everyone, "The whiter the bread, the sooner you're dead!" And there was a goblet of wine and I hadn't drunk alcohol, tea or coffee, for 15 years.

I'd been a fanatic about my health. It was like my whole belief system was there on the platter. I realised that it was more healing to be grateful for what he'd lovingly prepared for me, than for me to say, "I can't have what you've prepared because of my belief system." I thought, "Here I am on a mountain top in Italy, away from everyone I love. I know zip about anything". It was very, very humbling to be stripped bare. All that was left was gratitude for a complete stranger who had prepared a meal for me.

Ever since, I've wanted to pay my experience forward so that other people have a safe space in which to unravel and find their own meaningful pathway forward; this is why we now have the Quest for Life Centre in Bundanoon. Quest is a place where people are warmly welcomed into a safe environment in which they can utter the unutterable and have it witnessed and acknowledged by others. It is very powerful in people's healing process. Sometimes we don't know what we think until we hear what we say. It's only when we feel like someone 'gets' us, gets why we're feeling and acting the way we are, that we can move from a place of suffering to one where we feel more empowered.

Often, people try to haul us out of the emotional distress of our grief because bearing witness to our suffering is too uncomfortable a space for them. Many people hang on to their grief, their despair, their rage, their hopelessness, helplessness or powerlessness, until someone truly 'gets' them and accepts them wholeheartedly, the way they are. Then you may be open to seeing things differently. I think Father Llarino 'got' me, even though he didn't speak English and I didn't speak Italian. The simple fact of not understanding each other's words didn't stop us from speaking at length about life, love, music, God, loss and the purpose of human existence! A rich communication stream flowed from heart to heart, but it was never based on language. He was pivotal in my life. He was a quintessential Franciscan monk with a little round belly and wild fluffy white hair. While I ate whatever he'd prepared for me he would stand nearby with his fingers interlaced over his little round Franciscan belly watching me eat. He was determined that I should eat.

Karon: Why didn't you die after three months?

Petrea: Well, as I'm unsure as to why I developed leukaemia, I'm equally unsure of why I didn't die. I felt overwhelmed with a strong sense that I hadn't lived yet; I knew I hadn't done what I came here to do, even though I had no idea what that purpose was. That was one thing. The other overwhelming desire was to find peace; peace with myself, my history, my life. I think peace is actually a very powerful physiology in your body. Peace is not a passive, wishy-washy state of acceptance. It's a dynamic state of being where we feel able to embrace every moment regardless of its challenges with a quiet mind and an open heart. For instance, one day in the cave I realised, "There's nothing and no one to blame for my distress." That was incredibly disappointing as it had become a habit to blame people or circumstances for my distress!

I could still be sitting in that cave, a dusty pile of bones moaning about, 'it's not fair'. Why did I grow up with a brother like Brenden? Why did he tell me he was going to kill himself? Why years in hospital? Why rape? Why drugs? Why domestic violence? Why so much pain? But the simple fact was that all those things – and more – had happened. I wept buckets until I felt at peace. The exhaustion and tumult were great but finally, I was in a place where I could say, "Yes, all those things happened, but I refuse to be defined by the things that have happened to me." That's the challenge really, isn't it? Am I going to be defined by the traumas that have happened to me? Since then, in listening to over 120,000 precious stories of people's lives, I would say to anyone whose story I've heard, "You stay feeling as miserable, as depressed, as overwhelmed, as isolated and as grumpy as you need to for as long as you need to, because what happened to you is terrible." However, people recognise that won't lead to peace. We need to accept what has happened and allow it to carve deeply into our being so that we integrate the experience and are not emotionally crippled by the enormity of such suffering.

The challenge then becomes how will we find the heart to contain all of the anguish without losing our capacity to love? **I think there is an impetus towards healing and peace for most of us. It's often suffering that helps us to do that.**

Karon: You dedicated your book, *Quest for Life*, to Brenden because he taught you how to achieve peace. Can you tell us how he did that?

Petrea: Brenden's death catapulted me into self-blame for his suicide. Weeping the tears for the little girl who took on the responsibility for Brenden's life was a powerful and cathartic experience. I felt if I didn't get it right for Brenden, then he would die – and it would be my fault. I wept for the little girl who took on such an enormous responsibility that really wasn't hers, and I wept for Brenden. He and I both felt the pain of the world. We had so much in common; we were both compassionate and found the world a very confusing place. Then there were tears for the loss of Brenden. I'd never judge anyone who chooses to end their life. I knew and understood Brenden's pain. He did teach me a tremendous amount about what's important in life.

Karon: How did your family cope when Brenden died?

Petrea: We all grieved differently. My father had a lot of unresolved issues with Brenden and could never quite figure him out. There were times when Brenden was banished from the house due to his frustrating behaviours. My mother or I would surreptitiously let him in through a bedroom window, patch him up if necessary, give him a bowl of soup and some money, and he'd be out the window while my father, working quietly in his study, was oblivious to his comings and goings. I think my father's grief was more complex because he'd never really understood Brenden. My mother and I have always been close and meditation has been an important part of our lives. She and I took a more pragmatic but also spiritual view of Brenden's life and death although the manner in which he died, which was particularly violent, was very hard for both of us to come to terms with because he was such a passivist. My eldest brother, Ross, who is four years older than me, was terribly grief-stricken because he and Brenden were very close too. To this day, he prefers not to talk about Brenden's death and says, "It was such a waste." We all grieved in very different ways. Each person in our family had a strong, and in my father's case, often conflicted relationship with Brenden.

Karon: Suicide is certainly the most complex situation regarding loss for anyone to have to deal with.

Petrea: Absolutely. I could have been singing in the shower while he was going through his torment… thoughts like that shriek at you. How could I not know this was happening? He was too far away for any of us to have helped him.

Karon: There is usually a lot of guilt associated with suicide isn't there?

Petrea: Yes, and confusion. We knew Brenden had gone to the British Embassy for assistance. They had a function on that night and had said to him, "Come back to us tomorrow morning and we'll help you." That was the night that he took his life. His body had been cremated by the time dad was informed of his death. He told us some of the details around Brenden's death, and what he had done to himself was horrific. **What Geoff had described left us in shock and horror. What he didn't tell us left us with more questions and dreadful imaginings.** His words have reverberated down the decades.

I went to Kathmandu fourteen years after Brenden died. I wanted to breathe the mountain air and be in the atmosphere where he had been. I was completely unprepared for the onslaught of grief that engulfed me as the plane descended amongst these ancient mountains. I'd wept over Brenden's life and death. I'd talked about him. I'd written about him. Brenden was now an easy part of our conversation but as the plane landed, the lump in my throat halted all speech and I became a sobbing mess. No matter how hard I tried, I could not get words to form, let alone get them out of my mouth. Wendie, my partner, took over and spoke for me. I would not have believed this was possible if I hadn't experienced it. People say, if you don't grieve, you're likely to get a respiratory illness. Well, I went on to get pneumonia!

We had alerted the British Embassy before our departure from Australia, that we would like to visit and ask some questions. When we visited the Consul at the British Embassy where we knew Brenden had gone for help, Wendie again represented me as I still could not speak. When we emerged from the Embassy onto the tree-lined street, the entrance to that dreaded hotel was immediately opposite. My legs would not, could not walk into the hotel's grounds. The physical aspects of grief so often completely take you by surprise. **I felt hollowed out, amputated, dismembered.**

People don't understand the physical aspects of grief! We are more than our physical bodies; we know there's a whole electrical field that exists around our bodies. **When you love someone, their consciousness is enmeshed in yours, regardless of distance.** When it's ripped asunder, we go through a whole process of reidentifying who we are and what our place in the world, or our value in the world, might now become. We know who we are through our relationships and when those relationships are gone, we need to reinvent ourselves in new ways.

It wasn't until we were in Kathmandu that we found out that my father had made the decision to have Brenden's body cremated in Nepal rather than being sent home for burial. No doubt he wanted to ensure we never saw Brenden's body. However, the Consul told us that no one could possibly be cremated without the family's consent. It was a shock to find that my father had made this 'executive decision' without family consultation, though on reflection, this was also quite typical of his behaviour. While he was trying to protect us, my father left us with more questions than answers. In the decades after Brenden's death, these questions lurked in the background but could not be addressed as no-one dared confront any more reality.

We also visited the offices of the one English newspaper that was printed in Nepal. I wanted to see if there had been any report about a foreigner who had died in April of 1982. The staff were so kind and respectful but we found nothing relevant in any of the papers. When we walked down the rickety timber stairs from this five-storey building in Kathmandu and emerged into the sunshine, I felt a heaviness lift. I'd done what I could to find out any information and now, I would need to put it to rest because there were no answers.

Karon: Did you know where Brenden was cremated?

Petrea: Wendie asked the British Consul, "Could we visit the place where Brenden was cremated?" This man very diplomatically said, "It's not a very pleasant place these days." It was then he suggested we go to a very beautiful temple outside Kathmandu called Boudhanath and spend some quiet time there and perhaps purchase some prayer flags to take back to family members.

The ancient city of Boudhanath still hums with human traffic. The vast dome of the temple has the all-seeing eye on each of its four sides. As we began our journey to circumnavigate the dome, we were drawn to the first temple as it was full of Tibetan monks chanting, with long horns, drums and incense. We sat there for hours as this wonderful droning of the Tibetan monks drowned out all inner turmoil and grief. We purchased prayer flags to bring home, one of which still hangs faded and tattered in our garden. I've planted many trees in Brenden's memory. I think you go through so many rituals around grief to bring it home, to make it real. Now I'm comfortable with grief, but I think it's quite a journey for a lot of people as it certainly was for me. We grieve for a lifetime. Hopefully, we become more familiar with our own inner landscape of grief and less judgmental of it.

Karon: People need answers and you went to Kathmandu looking to fill in the gaps in Brenden's story. People don't seem to be able to let it go until they've got all the answers that are possible.

Petrea: **Once you get to that place where you have as much understanding of the circumstances as possible, you can move forward.** I think this applies to murder, accidents too, any number of losses. Certainly, I've had distressed fathers when their children have died from cancer asking, "Why did this happen to my son? How could this happen to my son? What did we do? Did we contribute in some way?" Those are terribly painful questions to ask yourself.

Karon: Those questions need to be addressed so you can let it go.

Petrea: Yes. Even with miscarriages, understanding why a miscarriage happened or whether it's preventable in the future, is all helpful information. So much expectation goes into a pregnancy. Then suddenly, due to a miscarriage, all those dreams are shattered. I know many women who've had multiple miscarriages. They often live in a perpetual state of grief and loss and a rollercoaster of emotions fuelled by hormones.

Karon: I believe women think, "Well, my body is meant to protect my child. Why wasn't it doing that?"

Petrea: Yes. Why did my body let me down with this cancer, this miscarriage, this chronic pain, this illness? Why did it do that? It can shake your sense of confidence in your own body.

Karon: You have a fascinating story. Did all these events motivate you to move towards the work that you're doing now?

Petrea: Absolutely! When you nearly die – and then you don't – you definitely know that happiness is not about the 'stuff' of life, having material possessions. **I realised that the only thing that really matters is love, the people in our lives and our relationships with them. Are you at peace with yourself? Are you at peace with your history? Are you at peace with the world?**

In the several months I spent in the cave, I found that peace and often it was through nature or such simple things. One day, I was in a morass of self-pity, shame and grief, marinating in misery. I was eating grapes while sitting in the beautiful forest surrounding the entrance to the cave when a beautiful blue and black butterfly landed on my knee. I squeezed a drop of grape juice for the butterfly and continued with my little pity-party. Lo and behold, another identical butterfly landed on my other knee. I squeezed it a drop of grape juice. Suddenly I realised I'm good for something; I'm a good place for butterflies to land on! That sounds pretty pathetic, but my self-esteem and sense of self was so abysmal at that time, I could see no purpose for my life. The butterflies gave me a little purpose. They drew me back to the moment instead of the inner torment in my mind. By the time I felt ready to return to Australia, I had found a good deal of peace. I wanted to be with my children and my family. If I was going to die, then so be it. I was at peace with dying; but more importantly, I was now at peace with living.

On my return to Australia, my GP repeated all the blood tests. We were both more than surprised when they showed my white blood cells within a normal healthy range and that I had a very high number of baby red blood cells. I certainly felt much stronger and healthier than when I'd left Australia, but I was as surprised, as he was by the results. The doctor said, "This remission you weren't meant to have, might only last a few days, maybe a few weeks." Paradoxically, I found that even more challenging than facing my mortality because, by then I had my whole life all packed up in this little suitcase ready for the big trip, then the plane got cancelled! I'd written my Will and my funeral. I'd made tapes and written letters for my children so they would know something of me in their future. I'd had all the long overdue conversations with my parents, and we were emotionally up to date with each other. When the 'plane' got cancelled, I was faced with the question, how much should I unpack? How do I live with any sense of confidence in life?

After about three months, my mother challenged me, "Have you thought of working, dear?" This came as such a shock. I had become so resolved with dying and living with uncertainty that I didn't know how to start my life again given the uncertainty of my remission. I knew Marcus Blackmore from my naturopathic study days, so I called to ask his advice. I blurted out to him, "Marcus, I'm meant to be dead from leukaemia, but I'm not. The doctor still says I'm going to die. He's not sure when. I'm a naturopath and a yoga and meditation teacher and I don't know what to do." It was Marcus who said, "Forget what the doctor said, go into practice." He introduced me to a GP in Mosman who was looking to share his practice, so I joined him. I didn't really want to be a naturopath. I'd found the whole journey of profound grief, the inner exploration of past painful traumas and the confrontation with my own mortality had been such an intense experience that being a naturopath didn't appeal to me. However, almost immediately, a woman with breast cancer came to see me. The day after, the first person with AIDS came to see me. Both Janine and John had been told they wouldn't see Christmas, which is what I'd been told 15 months before. I felt I'd met my tribe; people who lived in the land of uncertainty.

In the first decade, my work was mostly with people with cancer and AIDS, but they also brought stories of depression, anxiety, fear, domestic violence, sexual assault, relationship breakdown, grief, trauma, chronic pain and loss. We can't ever know what these experiences are like for another person, so it's never helpful to say, "I know exactly how you feel." I was, however, comfortable to have those conversations having gone through the whole exploration of my own inner terrain of unprocessed emotions. I was more than happy to listen as I had shared many of these same experiences. Sometimes we don't know what we think until we hear what we say. Having a safe space to utter the unutterable proved to be a powerful help for the people who came to see me.

I found their stories riveting. As they shared their secrets or their private anguish, I felt more and more comforted myself. I was not alone with the torments and struggles of being human. My life was no better or worse than anyone else's and the inner tumult I had experienced was a common anguish shared by many. Stories of suffering often confront us with the deeper questions about our own existence: who am I? What am I doing on the planet? Am I living the life I came here to live? If not, why not, and what am I going to do about it? I'd lived with those questions all my life and contemplated them deeply. My clients gradually helped me to find the words to describe the human experience of suffering and the blessed avenues that bring its relief.

Before long I started a voluntary massage program at St Vincent's Hospital for people with AIDS. At that time, staff were leaving patients' meals outside their doors for them to retrieve. I couldn't imagine how distressing it must be to feel so sick – and no one wants to touch you. I offered a weekly support and meditation group at Albion Street AIDS Clinic and then more groups in my home. For a decade, my children and I shared our home with up to 200 people each week who attended the ten different support and meditation groups I facilitated.

In 1989, I established the Quest for Life Foundation to further my work. I had always wanted to provide a safe space for other people to find their peace and healing, as I had been fortunate to have received Father Llarino's loving care. The precariousness of my health stopped me from following through on creating such a place as the last thing I wanted was to start something I couldn't complete.

Kay and her partner Wendie were in the very first cancer support group I facilitated in 1985. Kay had been diagnosed with breast cancer and her doctor had told her she would die within two years. Kay's three young teenagers were as distressed as Kay and Wendie were to be living with such a dark prognosis. I saw many people like Kay far outlive their doctors' expectations. Some people attained unexpected remissions while others are entirely free of their disease now, when that wasn't thought to be a possibility.

The people who sought my advice were keen to actively contribute to their own health or healing and their sense of wellbeing. They did many things to support their own health including dealing with unresolved emotional issues from the past, improving their nutrition, drinking fresh vegetable juices and increasing their exercise. They meditated and endeavoured to live a mindful life free of stress and strain. Kay lived for more than seven years and was a regular member of the support and meditation groups as well as seeing me for regular counselling. Before she died, she told Wendie, "When you're over the worst of the grief, go and see what you can do to support Petrea, because who looks after Petrea?"

Wendie wanted to take me to lunch or dinner to thank me for the care I'd taken of Kay. I usually didn't do this with clients or their family members because I'd had a few men transfer their affections from their wife to me! I had looked after their wife, often moving in for the last few days of a young mother's life, and occasionally a man would think I could be their new partner – and that surely wasn't going to work. However, I did have dinner with Wendie knowing that this wouldn't pose a problem! While we were having dinner, I felt like Wendie 'got' me, she got my life. She understood exactly because she'd been a part of some of the support groups during that time, but she understood why I lived the way I did because at that time, I worked seven days a week. My main priorities were to educate and care for my children for as long as possible and to do this work until I went out of remission. I fully expected I'd go out of remission sometime as my doctor was adamant that I would do so. It was Wendie who, some months later, said to me, "You know, you might not die, and you actually don't have a life," which came as a bit of a shock, but she was quite right in many ways. I'd spent what savings I had, and my parents had been supporting me while I was sick.

My daughter Kate had come back to live with me first, followed by my son Simon a couple of years later. I rented a large house so I could work in a home environment rather than a clinical environment. After all the trauma the children had experienced, I wanted them to come home and I would be there, even though I was working. The income from seeing clients paid the rent, educated the kids and kept us going. Many of my clients were unable to pay so much of my practice was pro bono. It was Wendie who really got me sorted. Within weeks of her volunteering, Wendie and I were inseparable. That's another story already told in my memoir! Wendie and I decided to move to Bundanoon in the Southern Highlands in 1995. I wasn't even sure that I'd continue doing this work because who'd come to Bundanoon?

The real estate agent who sold us our house was keen for me to see his daughter as she was in a remission from lymphoma. She was in her 30s and finding it difficult to reengage with life for the same reasons of feeling uncertain about having confidence in her body and not going out of remission. Wendie and I decided that from now on, our home would be our sacred sanctuary and that, if I was to continue doing this work, I'd need to find professional rooms. When I relayed this message to the man from the real estate office, he rang the next day and said, "I've got the rooms. Will you see my daughter now?" I rented half a house in Bundanoon and quickly, my practice took off again with barely a gap. The local motel in Bundanoon served as a venue for the weekend programs that I'd been conducting since my own recovery.

In 1998, a 35-bed guesthouse on nine acres came onto the market right in the heart of Bundanoon. I felt the property was meant for us, though I had no idea about how the Quest for Life Foundation might realise this dream. I was much better at giving things away than asking for help. Much to our delight, a benefactor made the funds possible for us to purchase and completely renovate the buildings to serve our purposes. Now, after 20 years, Quest conducts 30 five-day programs each year for people with physical illnesses or mental anguish due to grief, loss, trauma, depression, anxiety or posttraumatic stress injuries.

Karon: That is amazing. It sounds like you almost needed the life you had to be able to witness and be of service to these people because everything that happened in your life is now helping others, isn't it?

There is an important issue that I'd like to ask you about, and that's forgiveness. I think people often need to find forgiveness in their grief, and they find that very challenging.

Petrea: Forgiveness lies at the heart of so much around grief and, indeed, around everything in life. Some people hold onto the rage, the despair, the anguish of grief as a way of holding onto their loved-one believing that "If I forgive and let go, I am affirming that it was ok for them to die, and it was NOT ok." Sometimes people feel that, if they forgive, they'll be setting themselves up for being wounded again.

Forgiveness challenges us to find the heart that can contain our anguish without losing our capacity to love. Forgiveness is often misunderstood. The problem with not forgiving is that you continue to carry this wound, this heavy load, and it impinges on your joy and the possibility of peace. Forgiveness doesn't make it right, but it does set you free. Liberating ourselves from the angst of un-forgiveness sets us free to love, to live. When we choose to let go the baggage and we weep the tears and accept that this unimaginable loss happened, we begin the journey of healing or posttraumatic growth. "I'm no longer going to let it define who I am by taking up free rental space in my head." Forgiveness has nothing to do with the person or situation which offended us or caused us such pain. **Forgiveness is an inner process by which we liberate ourselves from the consequences of having felt wounded in the past.**

In this way, forgiveness is a selfish act. Why would we want to continue giving our power away to someone who wounded us? As someone said, "It's like wishing poison on the other person, but drinking it yourself." The other fabulous comment I heard about grief was at a conference in San Francisco, when a six-foot-five transsexual in a frock stood up a couple of seats along from me and said, "I've realised that forgiveness is giving up all hopes for a better past." I think self-forgiveness is often the hardest. It was definitely my greatest challenge – to forgive myself for not getting it right, for not being perfect, for not saving Brenden, for not saving the world, for not saving everything. As a child I'd taken on this huge responsibility and felt I'd failed so abysmally. We can weep about it, rail about it, scream about it, write about it, talk about it until its part of our story. Then we have a story, but we don't have to live from that story. It's good to have a story, because it is our story that breaks us open to greater compassion, hopefully to some small wisdom, we get clear about what our priorities are, who our friends are.

Being broken open through grief and through loss is very powerful and often transformative. We don't want to live as if that story is our only daily reality. We want to glean the wisdom from that story and take that into the future. I'm grateful for my story, because it helps me to meet people where they are, not because I know what it's like for them, but I know what my place of anguish, despair, hopelessness and powerlessness is. I'm happy to listen and bear witness to other people's stories. We don't want to live out of our story or keep blaming the past for who we are in the present. That's what we end up doing if we don't forgive. We keep blaming what happened in the past and use that as an excuse for why I am the way I am. That is a heavy burden to carry.

Karon: In the time you have seen 120,000 people, have you learned anything about how grief impacts on people's sexuality and need for intimacy?

Petrea: Yes, it's an interesting area, because I think that's a whole other chapter really. Grief doesn't always make a relationship better. There is a very high percentage of parents that separate after the death of a child. There can be all kinds of undercurrents present before the death of our loved-one which have never been addressed. Grief will blow everything unresolved out of the water. If you're not working on whatever those unresolved issues are in the relationship, then grief is pretty likely to shatter a relationship. Sometimes we want to stay in our misery, and we don't want intimacy to distract us from our pain. Some people use sex as a release from their pain, but it may well not be experienced as intimacy. This can cause all kinds of misunderstandings in a relationship and it becomes vitally important to find ways to talk about our feelings. Other people cling to each other and feel insecure and vulnerable when separated from the people who love and support them. Grief can bring a family together in new and more intimate ways but equally, can break a family apart.

In terms of intimacy in couples, grief is often dealt with so differently. One person can be having a 'good' day, and the other person doesn't want to bring them down, because they're not having a good day. Grief insists we face our emotional vulnerabilities. This is often very uncomfortable territory for people who were never taught how to be emotionally literate or articulate in their early years. For many people, the depth and power of grief takes them completely by surprise and catapults them into a new and unfamiliar emotional landscape. Some relationships have never had to go to that really vulnerable place. Grief brings some people solidly together, while it shatters others apart. This will depend on how much love there is in the relationship and how much commitment there is to working things through when difficulties come. **All I know is that what really matters in life is love.** If you're lucky enough to find someone who loves you and to whom you can give your love and that you have emotional vulnerability in your relationship, then that's a mighty precious thing.

Karon: Absolutely. You're lucky if it happens once in a lifetime. What does the future hold for Petrea King?

Petrea: **What gives me joy is seeing the lights come on in other people's eyes when they realise that they don't have to be trapped in whatever situation they're in; that they have choice.** Our work at Quest still gives Wendie and me great joy, because we've accomplished this together. We will continue to do our best to ensure Quest remains a sanctuary for people who need a compassionate space in which to begin or continue their healing journey.

Karon: Lovely. Thank you so much for all of your time, wisdom, openness, honesty and extensive experience.

Key Concepts

Petrea's story teaches us, if you deny your grief – and she had a backlog of unexpressed grief when young – it will come back at an unexpected time, usually with the trigger of another loss and flood your life.

We often need to make sense of what has happened and that can include going on a discovery journey until we can find no more answers. Then we can understand and tell our story or accept we have all the details possible.

What her father didn't tell the family about how Brenden took his life left them with more questions and dreadful imaginings. It is always better to know the truth, no matter what your age, because you can process the truth and accept it, but when there are gaps in the story people usually imagine the worst.

Trauma and suffering often confront us with the deeper questions about our own existence: Who am I? What am I doing on the planet? Am I living the life I came here to live? If not, why not, and what am I going to do about it? It's one of the gifts in loss.

There is a very high percentage of parents that separate after the death of a child. Bereaved people regress to between the ages of eight years to 13 years emotionally. Imagine children of that age trying to conduct a relationship. Also, both parents are bereaved at the same time so neither have much energy for the other or family responsibilities.

Things that helped Petrea's recovery:

1. Taking time out of her day to day life to focus on her needs after the leukemia diagnosis.

2. Petrea found letting out the years of accumulated grief in the cave appears to have given back her health.

3. Meditation and a healthy diet to support her body's needs.

4. Petrea found peace in going to Kathmandu to try and piece together what happened to her brother, Brenden when he suicided. We need the facts to understand and make sense of the story.

5. Accepting that being broken open through grief and loss is very powerful and often transformative.

6. Forgiveness is giving up all hopes for a better past. Petrea needed to forgive herself when she blamed herself for Brenden's death.

7. Refusing to be defined by the things that have happened to her.

8. Hearing others stories comforted Petrea, as she recognised, she was not alone with the torments and struggles of being human. Being with others who have had similar experiences can be very reassuring. That's why groups work so well.

9. Recognising that what really matters in life is love.

10. Paying her experience forward so that other people have a safe space in which to unravel and find their own meaningful pathway forward.

11. Creating a legacy, the Quest for Life Foundation, to offer that healing space to others became her life work and has given her a rewarding and meaningful life.

Chapter 2

James Thomas

FEEL THE MAGIC

"The purpose of life is not to be happy at all. It is to be useful, to be honourable. It is to be compassionate. It is to matter, to have it make some difference that you lived."

Leo Rosten

James and Kristy Thomas | Photo by Clifford Jansz

JAMES THOMAS Biography

Co-founder Feel the Magic

As a young entrepreneur, James ran his own business and was an active property investor committed to living a successful life. In the wake of losing his parents, James realised the life he had created was unfulfilling and unrewarding. Driven from his own grief and heartbreak, he decided he wanted to leave his mark on this world whilst honouring the memory of his mum and dad.

James has since dedicated his life to supporting the overall mental health and emotional wellbeing of bereaved Australian children and teens. He and his wife Kristy brought Feel the Magic to life.

Feel the Magic is an Australian charity with three key objectives,

1. Provide a safe place to grieve.

2. Provide the age appropriate tools to heal.

3. Create 'MAGIC' through the power of human connection.

Grieving children who have experienced the death of someone they love can feel isolated and alone. They require ongoing support in developing strategies to cope with and move forward with their lives following a significant loss. Feel the Magic provides grief education and support to bereaved children, teens and their families to help alleviate the pain and isolation felt by the loss of a parent, sibling or legal guardian.

James greatest achievement is becoming a father. Together with his beautiful wife Kristy, they love spending time with their boys Madden and Chase as a family.

James strives to share his passion whilst sharing his story and inspire others to chase their dreams, being an example of living a life filled with purpose despite the many challenges of life.

The Interview

Karon: James, what motivated you to create this wonderful organisation, Feel the Magic.

James: When I was 25, I lost my dad to a two-year cancer battle. Until then, I had been living for the weekend, had no real drive or purpose. Dad's passing was the catalyst for change because it forced me to grow up! I was an only child and I wanted to take care of my now widowed mother. Dad's death gave me a purpose! It made me realise that I needed to do something with my life. That's why I actually sat down and wrote a goal to buy or build a dream home in a beautiful part of Sydney that would house Kristy, my girlfriend at the time, and now my wife, our future family and my mother. When I made that decision, I realised I needed to earn a lot more money and I needed to be a bit more strategic about, how I could achieve that goal? With a signage background, I started my own business, I worked very hard and was on the path of creating financial security.

To justify my existence, I was spending money like I needed to fulfill something, because I had no life. I was working seven days a week, sometimes 24 hours a day to achieve that ultimate goal. I wanted to make my mum proud that she had a house and a roof over her head and we could support her in her later years of life. That was 2005. By December 2010, we put a deposit on a house in Pitt Town NSW, but we couldn't move into it for another six months because it was a display home in a new estate. We were moving from a three-bedroom home to a six-bedroom home, so we had to fill it with furniture. I worked my backside off to buy more material things. On my 31st birthday, and within hours of picking up the keys with friends and family locked in to help us move, my mum dropped dead from a brain aneurysm.

Karon: Oh, my goodness. That's a rupture of a blood vessel and bleeding into her brain isn't it?

James: Yes. Completely out of the blue. My grandparents lived well into their 90s. Mum was only 72, very fit and healthy, she looked about 52. I was in shock and overwhelmed from losing her. **Even though I was a 31-year-old man, I felt like a young orphan that had no one to turn to. That was a life-changing experience. I felt ripped off, ashamed, guilty, I felt all these things that tend to come with grief.** One thing I didn't realise is that I wasn't grieving, as silly as that sounds. The way I grieved Dad's death was to find purpose at Dad's funeral and I went into action. **When Mum died, I wanted to get into action to get over it. But because I was trying to avoid it and get over it, the darkest part of my grief lasted probably two years. It was the darkest two years of my life.** Burying Mum was very difficult. I don't really remember it as I was in so much shock. I felt I was in a position where no one understood me because I didn't know anyone else in my situation. All my friends still had their parents, my wife had her parents. No one really knew what to say to me and if they did, they usually said the wrong thing like, "She's in a better place now," or, "Things happen for a reason."

Karon: All the platitudes.

James: Yes. When they'd say that, I'd think, no, she's not in a better place. A better place was here. This was a new beginning she was excited about. The sad thing is she never stepped a foot in our house. That was a gaping big hole in my life personally and for my wife as well. The best thing that was explained to me at the time was grief is like a puzzle. Once you take a key component of that puzzle, all these other pieces fall away. That's how I found my life. **Everything was falling away, I felt really anxious and lost and deeply saddened by what I was going through and not knowing how to deal with it.** I tried to avoid it. At the eight-month mark, I was sleeping and woke up two hours before my alarm clock with this question. "If I died tomorrow, would I be happy with the life that I've created?" We had this beautiful house. We had a business that was doing okay. Money wasn't really an issue. My wife was at university, I was working full time and we were living comfortably. We had this financial security, but I wasn't proud of it. It was a huge dent to my ego. When I started making all this money, I honestly thought life was easy. I thought you work hard and things fall into place and the rest takes care of itself. It was probably the first bit of trauma that I experienced in my life that affected me badly.

Karon: Because it was so sudden and unexpected?

James: Sudden and it was my last parent. There's research now that shows that when you lose both your parents it's completely different. Even now when my wife's not having a good day or she needs support, she rings her parents up. I look at that and go, **"Wow, you are so lucky to do that because I can't do that anymore. I haven't been able to for eight years."** It's a difficult one. I remember that was such a profound moment in my life where it really made me question 'what am I doing?' I couldn't find purpose in building this financial security. I think for the first time I could say, maybe Mum did die for a reason. I think that was quite a profound moment in my life. Being me, I went back to work, and got busier and busier. I pushed aside my own emotional needs and I developed a hatred for my work. I really...

Karon: Resented it?

James: Resented it big time. Getting out of bed was a struggle. Sometimes I'd shed a tear trying to get out of bed to get to work. I couldn't deal with people because no one understood what I was going through. I wouldn't verbalise it either. It was hard when I was bottling up these emotions with no outlet or permission. Not that I couldn't do it with my wife, but there's only so much you can unload on your wife or your loved ones. I did resent the business and was wanting it to fold. I didn't want to be there anymore. Six months had passed and my wife, as good wives do, sat me down and said, "You know I love you. We've been through hell and back. This has been a really tough experience. I've supported you. I'll continue to support you, but you have to start looking after yourself, supporting yourself because if you don't, I'm not going to be here anymore." She was another person in my life that I didn't want to lose. I remember throwing my hands in the air saying, "What do you want me to do? What do I do?" She said, "I think you need to sell your business because it's killing you." I wanted to fight her because I thought how are we going to keep the houses? How are we going to do this? How are we going to survive? But at the same time, it was like this huge weight was lifted off my shoulders. I think unconsciously I knew she was right. The next day, I went to work and spoke to one of my staff members asking, "Would you like to buy my share?" She said, "I would love to, leave it with me." It was about a month later, December 9, my share of the business was sold and I was out of there. I was a free man.

At the time, it was very stressful because the business wasn't going well. I had lost my focus, passion and drive. The business is thriving now and the new owner is succeeding in her own right. A week later on the 16 of December 2012, we flew to America for a month. Part of the itinerary was Disneyland. I didn't want to go but my wife made me go. But it's probably been one of the best places I've ever been to and I'm so thankful for the experience because it was there that Feel the Magic was discovered. It was the first time ever in my life I've never had a job or a business or income. Going over there, I let go, and what's the old saying, "Let go and let God." I thought if something's meant to be, something will happen when I get back. I'm going to go enjoy this holiday. Going to Disneyland, I felt freedom that I hadn't felt for most of my life. It was the first time I actually felt and gave permission for my parents to be with me. It took me way back to my childhood watching Disney movies and remembering some of the characters and songs I had completely forgotten about. It reminded me of sitting on a lounge with my feet not touching the floor and Mum and Dad at my side watching movies. I knew I was in the right place at the right time in that moment. I felt happy and was thinking wow, this is great.

I'm a big daydreamer. Day two of Disneyland, I remember sitting, eating lunch and looking at all the kids and they were in the moment, having fun wearing their character masks. I was so taken aback by how present they were in their surroundings. Whereas I was always about, "I need to buy this investment product because this will set us up for the future, we need to run a successful business, we need to set up financial security because it'll pay for our way in the future," rather than being in the moment and being present and happy. It was right then and there when I was in the moment that I was hit over the head with this idea, what if I raised money and sent kids from Australia to the happiest place on earth, Disneyland? I remember turning to my wife saying, "I have this idea, what do you think?" She said, "Oh, it's a great idea. Let's look at it when we get back." That was January 2013 and by 18 July 2013, we were a fully-fledged, not-for-profit organisation. We had stumbled and fumbled our way into becoming a charity. I didn't really have an intention of becoming a charity, all I wanted to do was raise money to send kids who have lost a mum or dad or a sibling to the happiest place on earth. It went from that to sending 12 or 13 families. We noticed that the families were reaching out to one another and connecting, supporting one another through the tough times, they all got it.

Disneyland is great, it's fantastic, but it's a Band-Aid solution. **It's not there to give the tools necessary to thrive from grief.** We looked into what we could do further. We researched what was in Australia and there was hardly anything. We wanted something more impactful, more kids and more interaction with one another. My wife, our friend Peter Maloney, his sister Anne Mills, and I put our heads together and created a program called Camp Magic. In America there is a grief camp for kids and Peter and I flew over and took part in their program. I was matched with a little boy who lost his dad in gang violence. He was shot point-blank in the head in a drug deal gone wrong. As an Australian, it blew my mind to hear that from an eight-year-old boy. I was like, wow, that's some heavy, heavy stuff that he needs to live with, right?

Karon: Yes, so traumatic.

James: Every adult had a child camper with a grief counsellor in age-appropriate groups to talk about the kid's loss and how us mentors, big buddies, have experienced loss. It was fantastic and it was a great experience. We came back and kept working with our Camp Magic model, creating a safe place for grieving kids to grow. We support kids between the ages of seven to 17 years of age who have lost a parent, sibling, or legal guardian. We hold 'Talk Time', based on the metaphor of seasons. **Each season represents a stage of their grief. Autumn represents change, when someone passes away. Winter is when the grief really hits, you're sad, you can't see a light at the end of the tunnel. Spring, things are a little bit better, now you're starting to feel a bit more normal. Summer is warm, it's fuzzy and you're feeling hope.** No matter what stage of the season they're at, if their loved one died, let's say on Christmas Day, if they're feeling sad that morning, they've got the tools that they learned in the winter phase to get them through that phase rather than going, "I don't know what's wrong with me," and suppressing those emotions.

There are fun activities, confidence building, team building activities that bring these kids together who wouldn't meet in the normal world. The program's been built on four values, empathy, empowerment, growth, connection. Empathy is the key because we empathise with these kids; we don't feel sorry for them. I guess when you hear someone who loses a dad or a brother or sister, you go, "Oh that poor kid." The kid doesn't want your pity, they need empathy because they still need boundaries, they still need to get on with their life, but they also need to learn how to grieve in a healthy way and that's what we provide. We empower these kids to grieve and learn the tools necessary. Once they learn those tools, they grow as an individual because they feel like they're dealing with the most difficult thing they're ever going to have to deal with. It's about growing as a human being and connection where we can have kids from all over the country that can come together. **Grieving kids do generally feel like they're the only person in the world that's going through it.**

We're now running a Parent and Guardian Workshop. We realised that parents were dropping their kids off, and the kids were having a life-changing experience, then going home into the same environment and the parent didn't know what was going on. Now when the parents drop the kids off, they come to a parent workshop, which is a four-hour session broken in two where they are provided the tools and the dialogue so they can understand what the children are learning. When they go home together as a family, they can support one another through their grief.

Karon: Fantastic. I know that children do well if their parents are doing well. Can you summarise what you know about the acute stage of children's grieving? The immediate three to six months after the loss.

James: We don't have any kids come in our program unless its six months post the death. For some kids, it's the shock. It's the disbelief and they're supported in that first six-month period. There's friends and family. Family comes from interstate; all the world comes to support that family. For kids, it hasn't really hit because they're still supported and their life, as they knew, hasn't reformed yet. When everyone moves on with their life because they think the child or family is doing okay. That's when grief really hits them. That's when they need the tools and the understanding and the support network that understands what they're going through. When someone's stoic and seemingly handling their loss really well, our society thinks they're doing great. When someone is a blubbering mess on the floor, we think they're struggling. The opposite is true. They are expressing their pain.

Karon: I often hear, "She wasn't even crying at the funeral." My thought is she was in shock, that's why she wasn't crying. But the implication is, "Oh she's so strong." People actually say, "So strong, she wasn't crying."

James: Yes, it's not about being strong. **A lot of children develop separation anxiety because when one parent is gone, they worry what's going to happen to the other parent?** There is that attachment. Sleeping becomes an issue. They don't want to sleep alone in case something happens to the parent. That's quite a common reaction.

Karon: I think some people are surprised when children can be in the moment and playing and having fun whereas adults tend to be grieving most of the time and not able to give themselves permission to have fun.

James: A lot of kids are different, but they can connect with like-minded children. They don't even necessarily have to talk about it. If they know that someone else has experienced loss like they have, they feel normal again and they feel like they've got someone who gets it on a much deeper level than someone who hasn't gone through it. **Talking about it, drawing, doing a photo book, art therapy, that's always a great way for kids to express how they're feeling in that moment.** Talking about the loved one because... there's a quote I heard recently, "A man is only dead when he's forgotten," which I thought was quite profound, because you don't want these kids to forget their lost loved one. They need to talk about funny stories with their family. The more they can keep that person alive in their heart and their mind, the better off they're going to be.

Karon: What behaviours can adults look out for in grieving children that might be a concern?

James: Becoming withdrawn, aggressive and angry, or teenagers locking themselves in their room. There's emotional eating, but that's a coping strategy, that's okay. They tend to grow out of that. I would say becoming withdrawn or angry and refusing to talk about it. I think that can be quite a concern if a child refuses to talk about it because eventually it's going to come out otherwise.

Karon: What can an adult do if they see these behaviours?

James: Look, you can't force them to talk about it. As an adult, I feel like they need to look out for themselves number one, and the child will eventually follow. A parent needs to lead the way. Seeking a support network, celebrating the birthday of the person who has died, celebrating the Christmases, acknowledging that they existed. It is difficult with teenagers because they tend to not listen to their parents or parent. But if there's someone that they can trust and know the child will listen to, they can act as a mentor to the child.

Karon: I know it's common for children to blame themselves for the loss or death of someone, which can result in guilt. Can you tell me about the thought's children might have blaming themselves for the loss? Some of the things you've heard?

James: Yes, some of the things we've heard is, "I want to kill myself so I can go and be with them in heaven." In the event of suicide, "If only I didn't go to school that day, I would have been able to save them." "Had I not been a naughty child, my parent would still be here." Innocent things. **There are many ways a child blames themselves because the child's world revolves around them. When a big piece of their world is taken away it's their fault in their mind.**

Karon: If a child is keeping their feelings a secret because of the guilt they feel, how can adults go about trying to find out why the child may be blaming themselves.

James: It's a good question. How would they find out? I honestly think it goes back to the parent getting themselves right and getting the tools necessary to support their children because a child can't blame the other parent if they have an open, honest relationship. There are great stories of children blaming the person who's delivered the message. If the other parent said, "Your dad's dead," that child will blame that parent. It's, don't shoot the messenger. It's almost better to get someone that is not so connected to the family to deliver that message. But in terms of them blaming themselves, I think its reiteration that it's not their fault. The more they look out for themselves, the safer the home space is going to be. Not playing into the guilt trips. Far too often we see kids that are using it as an excuse when they are in trouble. **The parent goes softly with them when they should be reprimanded and disciplined in a way that's according to the act that they've done. Children need boundaries.** Unfortunately, it all falls on the parent's shoulders. A child's going to believe what they believe, but its positive reinforcement all the time from the parent. But if you're in a state of you're feeling guilty or if you're feeling like you're not dealing with your own grief, it's hard to be aware. **The number one thing is to be really aware of the child's self-talk and what they're actually talking about, and being honest about the loss and why their parent or their sibling isn't here.**

Karon: Have you worked with children who weren't told the truth, who didn't get the chance to say their goodbyes or weren't included in the funeral, and what did they say about that?

James: Yes, we have. There's still that stigma around suicide and some families believe the child is better off not knowing. We've had kids whose parent says, "We haven't told him that their mother or father suicided, can you please not tell them?" It really throws a spanner in the works for us because we need to be open and transparent. **We encourage the parent to tell the child the truth. They need to know. If you keep it from them, they have to revisit that whole grieving period with the truth.**

Karon: That would make it incredibly difficult for them because they're going to find out at some stage.

James: **Honesty is the best policy when it comes to a loss** whether it's suicide or cancer, whatever it may be. We've actually had a counsellor advise their patient to tell us not to talk about suicide in our programs. That's ridiculous because suicide has such a high death rate in Australia. Why wouldn't you want that child to know? Potentially, they can look after themselves growing up, and I know that there's other people out there that will get it and understand and want to talk about it with them.

Karon: How does the psychological wellbeing of the surviving parent impact the child's grief?

James: Big time because a child needs to feel safe, whether that's from one parent or two parents or the whole family. The child needs to know that they're safe in their home environment, especially the younger years. Things need to be routine still, school, bedtimes, and meals, whatever it may be. It's when they start going outside those boundaries because the parent isn't looking after themselves, things start to fall through the cracks. Homework not getting done, not going to bed on time, more screen time than usual. That's when they start developing guilt trips, "I want my screens, my dad died," and it's a gateway to creating a victim mentality for that child.

Karon: For the rest of their life?

James: Yes, it's a hard one to get rid of if you're a victim. It's of the highest importance that parents grieve, they need to grieve and it's not about being stoic. They need to be vulnerable and honest, and say, "Today I'm having a bad day because I'm missing your dad or your mum," and have a cry together. It's not about trying to be tough and strong in front of your child. **You want to show that some days are going to be crap, some days are going to be fantastic and life will go on and life will be safe. That's all the child wants to know.**

Karon: If there's valid blame associated with the death and the example you gave before would be one of those, how do you work with children needing to find forgiveness?

James: It's a good question. It's about them identifying why they blame and what it is about the blame and replacing that with a positive act. For example, we ask the kids to list how they deal with their grief in a negative way and how they deal with their grief in a positive way. Then you can see the similarities and what they really love to do. It's about focusing on what they love to do and using that whenever they feel like they need to blame someone. We've got a number of tools. I guess for me, I don't deliver the tools. I run the business, Kristy, who is the National Program Coordinator could probably answer that one a bit better than me.

Kristy: We don't specifically look at individual cases. What we would do is, through our different activities, work out what they're actually feeling. If it is blame, it would probably come out as anger or frustration. Then we work individually on the actual feeling itself, giving the child ways to recognise when they're feeling it and then what to do with that. Rather than actually talking through that anger of, "I feel angry because of all this," it's recognising okay, when you feel that, what is associated with that feeling, how can you then move on from that? Every child that's sitting in the room has a different story. Working out how they're feeling rather than the actual story is what we work with.

Karon: Would you discuss how children's grief impacts on them over their lifetime?

Kristy: It's a very broad question but I'll run through as many as I can think of. It usually and generally can really affect them socially within their peer group for many reasons but often, they can feel quite jealous that their peers still have their parents or siblings, because they can noticeably see what they're missing out on. Socially, they can become quite ostracised and bullying is something that they actually experience quite often. Because they feel isolated, a lot of children think that they're the only person going through it. That isolation can affect their confidence, their self-esteem, their wellbeing, in a general way.

James: It can also lead to severe mental health problems. If a child is not addressing everything Kristy mentioned and they're generally living with that and not dealing with that, then there's no doubt that they're going to go down that road of mental health later in life. They can develop addictions, they can develop bad behaviours, bad habits.

Kristy: **One of the things that's very prevalent in a grieving child is anxiety.** They become extremely anxious about the world not being safe, for obvious reasons. Separation anxiety can impact their life because they don't want the remaining parent to leave them. That can affect their social life because they don't go and stay anywhere, they don't feel comfortable going to school camp. Often coming to Camp Magic can be the first time they've spent time away from the other parent. That's one thing that definitely is very prevalent. Then depending on the level of trauma that they've gone through, associated with the deaths, for example murder. Or if they were present at the time. We've had plenty of kids who have found the parent or guardian dead. The level of trauma can really impact their learning. It affects the part of their brain that has anything to do with learning and they really struggle at school.

Karon: How often can they go to Camp Magic?

Kristy: They can go as often as we can possibly fit them in. We don't really have a set minimum amount. There are some children that come to camp and you know that they need it more than others, so they'll come more often. Then there are some kids that come once and get what they need but they create this new community that they're still a part of. Then you get kids that come once or twice a year to have that top up and reconnect with friends. It can really vary for every child about how many times they come. For instance, we had this beautiful teenage boy who arrived at camp for his first time, I looked at him and thought, "Oh my gosh, this child." You could tell he was so uncomfortable and his eyes were downcast. Lost both parents at different times, lives with an aunt but has a severely disabled sibling as well. Another level of responsibility going on there. After camp, he had such a huge turn around that we said straight away, "This is the type of child that needs a regular visit."

Kristy: He said at the end of camp, "This is the best fun I've had in years," and he's had no friends, he gets bullied.

Karon: I can't believe they get bullied.

Kristy: Oh, they do. Kids can be so cruel. They can also be cruel without meaning to be. For instance, we've got a mentor who has a son that also comes to camp, so they come at different times. She was saying that her son was buying a Father's Day present at school and another kid said, "Why are you buying a present if you don't have a dad?" But because he's very well equipped, he said, "I do have a dad. He's in heaven so I'm still buying him a gift." But for another child that could be absolutely devastating to be confronted with, "Oh, you don't have a dad?" Which lots of kids do say, or they're even asking, "How come you don't have a dad? Where's your dad?" To a child, it's so unbelievable that a child doesn't have a mum or dad. Sometimes it's a child being so blown away by the fact that a child cannot have a dad because he died.

Kristy: If you've got something that's a little different, they'll pick up on it.

James: Kristy's older brother Cory died when they were kids, due to leukemia. Kristy was bereaved as a child.

Karon: Were you well supported Kristy?

Kristy: I think I had a fantastic family, a supportive family in that it was never a secret. We talked about it. I knew who he was and always knew lots of stories and things about him. For me it didn't come out till I was about 19, 20 years when I started to feel the effects and had to seek some professional help because I didn't know how to deal with it. I also didn't know, because I was so young, how to pinpoint what was going on. Then I started to realise, "That did have a huge impact on my life." He was my best friend. When I reflect back on my life, I think oh, yes, I've always struggled to keep friends because I've always had that fear that they're going to leave. You don't realise how it shapes your life until you become a bit older and wiser. It affected me later in life, around the time I had children too.

Karon: Because of your fears about your children dying?

Kristy: I think it was the realisation of what my parents went through. My mum suffered badly from depression, for a good four years. She was in bed. I guess looking at my own child and thinking, "Oh, okay, I get it."

Karon: How you would feel if your child died?

Kristy: How I would feel, yes.

Karon: However, it's not good for the children to have a dysfunctional parent and in that situation, you can have two dysfunctional parents.

Kristy: Thankfully, I think Dad sort of held the fort around that time but when Mum got better, Dad broke down. They came good later in life but, I don't know how they'll ever get over that. I think he's also shut out a lot of what's happened because I can sit with Mum for hours and she'll tell me stories of this happened and that happened. Every year on the anniversary of his death, she'll tell me the whole story, from start to finish, of the day that he died. Sometimes I'll tell Dad things and he will say, "I didn't know that." He doesn't remember. That is two very different perspectives.

James: I think it's probably two different approaches to dealing with it too.

Kristy: For sure. Depending on your personality as well and how much help you get.

Karon: Do you have any golden rules for adults in dealing with their children who are grieving?

James: **Being completely transparent and honest, no matter how much it hurts** because we see the hurt on the children's faces when they don't know all the information. There's one girl that springs to mind that didn't know her dad committed suicide. It was like she was grieving a lie and then found out the truth and then there was this mess.

Kristy: **But it's still a mess because a child knows they haven't got all the information. They know energetically. When they don't have it all, that's when it spirals. For them they can internalise it, "Was it me? Did I do something?"**

Karon: Because it doesn't make sense and we need to make sense out of the loss. Don't we?

Kristy: Especially a child. They need to do it as simply as possible, but they need all the information, no secrets.

James: One of our ambassadors told the story that her mum died when she was ten years old and no one told her how. Then when she was 30 years old, she found out her mum committed suicide and she re-grieved.

Karon: She had to go back in time and re-grieve with the truth.

James: Her dad asked, "What's the matter?" She said, "Dad, I feel like I've lost Mum all over again." "If I'd known back then, I would have dealt with it back then."

Kristy: I had a teenager in my last group at camp who had attended camp previously. She was 13 years old and she knew there was some information that she wasn't getting and it prompted her to have the ability to actually go ahead and say, "Mum, I know you're not telling me everything, can you tell me everything? I need to know." Her mum did share the details of what had happened. She had withheld information to protect her but in fact; it was eating away at her. As soon as the girl knew, she became closer to her mum and their relationship healed. So, when she came back to camp the second time, she had such a better outlook on what was going on because she had all the information.

Karon: I guess, if you're keeping a secret from someone, you can't be open in a relationship. You need to always be aware of keeping that secret.

James: You can't be transparent yourself. How do you expect a child to be open and transparent and live a happy, healthy life if you're closing it?

Kristy: **Then there's always that fear they are going to overhear something? I've heard of kids finding out stuff at school because another parent knows, and they've told their child and then it comes back to the grieving child the other way.**

Karon: That's a bad way to find out, isn't it? In the school playground.

James: For sure. That's another different trauma.

Karon: You know how children worry about the remaining parent dying. How do you deal with that or give them the tools to feel safe in the world around that?

Kristy: Well, it's so common they feel that and it is something they have to work really hard to overcome because it is a real fear. It's not a made-up fear.

Karon: Because no one can guarantee the other parent won't die?

Kristy: **No one can guarantee. It's not like you can say to the child, "I'm not going anywhere." We help them to realise that loss is part**

of life and it's a natural occurrence in life and you can't be scared of it, because it's inevitable. The only way we see we can do that, is by building their resilience in feeling safer in the world. It's the only way because there's no guarantees unfortunately.

Karon: I guess if they see their parent looking after their health that would be a good thing.

Kristy: Definitely. I think it starts with the child if they're looking after themselves emotionally too. We help them to realise that they've got to look after themselves and that the parent looks after themselves so they can both be together. If the child feels responsible for the parents' happiness and health which is very common, they don't want to mention anything or bring up anything because they don't want to hurt their parents. Give them that ability to still speak out regardless of the reaction of what they're going to get from the parent and often that opens the communication for them because the child is not worried about how the parents are going to react.

Karon: It really does sound like you're building amazing resilience in these kids.

Kristy: Yes, absolutely. As we say to them, "You've probably been through the worst thing you're ever going to go through. At the end of the day, these kids become stronger than other kids because they've had to deal with this when they're younger. They grow up a lot quicker too. At least 90% of our teens take on more responsibilities in the household because…

Karon: They have to, don't they? Because there's a parent missing who used to do things.

Kristy: Yes. If they can recognise that as a positive thing, instead of, "Ah, it's not fair I'm doing this," it's this is part of my life. That does build their resilience to go, "You know what, I am strong, and I can do this." It's tricky though.

Karon: How does the love and support of close relatives and friends, of the family impact on the children's grief? What can those people do to support the child and the bereaved parent?

Kristy: It's so important, never go away. Keep being there.

James: **And understand there's not a time, there's not a timeframe on grief.**

Kristy: Understand that some people will never stop grieving, and some people will seemingly get on with their life within months, a year, two years. But never stop being there regardless of how you think they're going because, there's no timeline. What we hear and what we've experienced from dealing with so many families are the first three months everyone's involved, everyone's calling, dropping food off, helping with getting the kids to school. Then at six months that sort of drops off a bit but still people are calling and checking in.

By the 12-month mark there's no one. Everyone's gone back to their own life and literally they're on their own. **My advice is be there for that 12-month mark; continue being there and then two years from there, still offer to take the kids to school because the parent will still be running that rat race on their own.**

James: Young people need that extra person they look to, that they can tell anything to. In our cases, that's why they connect with their mentors because they can say what they want to say. They can find them in the outside world, outside of their parents, that's our deal. Aunties and uncles need to step up.

Kristy: What we have experienced is there are a lot of families that lose family afterwards. I don't know how many times I've heard a bereaved parent say, "I've lost family as well."

Karon: You mean they stop being a part of their family?

Kristy: Yes. The bereaved wife, who lost her husband, his family sort of falls away. It doesn't feel part of the family anymore. And there's the kids and…

Karon: They're dealing with their own grief of losing their child.

Kristy: Sure. You can't imagine it, can't you?

Karon: If I were a grandparent, I would want to continue seeing the child.

Kristy: I would be there every day. I'd be making sure that my son or my daughter's kids were feeling loved and supported.

James: There are many reasons, money is one of them. Sometimes families fall out over who's getting what and they walk away. Sometimes it's too hard for them to look their grandkids in their face because it reminds them of who they've lost. Let's say they're not dealing with their own grief. Not only are they avoiding theirs, that child misses out again.

Kristy: But then I can say the ones that have hung around, offering good family support, we can tell there's a difference in the child.

Karon: They do much better?

James: Definitely.

Karon: Thank you so much for your time and for sharing your experience in supporting children through their grief journey. Feel the Magic is awesome.

Key Concepts

No matter the age of your parents, when they are both dead you will feel like an orphan. It changes you forever, particularly if you are an only child. You can feel anchorless. Some people describe it as having your roots taken away. You can be left feeling alone even though you have your own family and friends. Or you can feel jealous, envious of others who still have their parents.

You tend to get through the grief and you'll probably get used to it, but you don't get over it. A piece of your life jigsaw has been removed and the pieces never quite fit in the same way again.

If a child loses one or both parents, they need stability in their life, boundaries and good solid ongoing support for years. They would benefit enormously from attending Feel the Magic camps.

Things that helped James's recovery:

1. After his dad's death James realised that he needed to do something with his life. He found a purpose and created a goal to purchase a home.

2. After his mum's death he was profoundly affected and tried to push his grief away but he recognised he needed to give it its rightful place.

3. Selling his business when he had lost his passion for it freed him up to think about what he wanted to do with his life and he co-created Feel the Magic to support kids who had lost a parent. He had empathy for them because of his own experience of losing his parents.

4. Having his own family. James feels his greatest achievement is becoming a father. Together with his beautiful wife Kristy, they love spending time with their boys Madden and Chase as a family.

5. Dedicating his life to supporting the overall mental health and emotional wellbeing of bereaved Australian children and teens.

6. Inspiring others to chase their dreams, being an example of living a life filled with purpose despite the many challenges of life.

7. Creating this legacy from his own experience has helped him see his parent's deaths as having meaning.

The most beautiful people we have known are those who have known defeat, known suffering, known struggle, known loss, and have found their way out of the depths.

These persons have an appreciation, a sensitivity, and an understanding of life that fills them with compassion, gentleness, and a deep loving concern.
Beautiful people do not just happen.

Elisabeth Kübler-Ross

Chapter 3

Louis Reed

"Learn to get in touch with the silence within yourself and know that everything in this life has a purpose. There are no mistakes, no coincidences. All events are blessings given to us to learn from."

Elisabeth Kübler-Ross

LOUIS REED Biography

Lou Reed

Energy Shaman

Founder – Integrative Medicine Institute (IMI) and Tribal News TV

Creator of – Soul Psychology, Art Psychology, Energy Psychology

---

Founder of Integrative Medicine Institute an online campus for all things regular schooling forgot to teach you. We specialise in Energy Psychology, a powerful method that creates shifts in your consciousness, transforming all dimensions of your being: mind, body, soul and human connection.

Lou reflects the wholeness of the human experience by combining, Art and Science to align your three levels of consciousness bringing you back into alignment with the unique story of YOU, your living masterpiece. Your life is your Art! Nothing will satisfy you more than creating your world from the song of your heartbeat.

You are not alone; there are energy creative warriors out there who feel things deeply and want to make a difference with their story. One act of courage at a time. www.integrativemedicine.institute

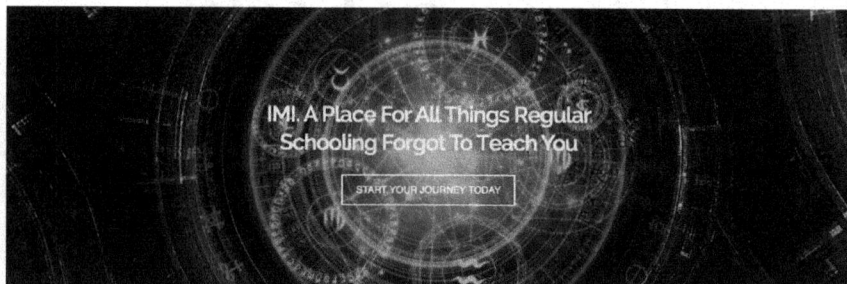

IMI. A Place For All Things Regular Schooling Forgot To Teach You

START YOUR JOURNEY TODAY

The Interview

Karon: Lou Reed, lovely to interview you and thank you so much for your time.

Louis: I am so excited to be part of this project. You're writing a book that I feel will change people's lives and it's creating sustainable generational change. As people change their way of being in the world, they start to model it differently to their children, so their children learn differently and then their children's children. I feel it's such a wonderful gift to leave the planet, because grief is not something that we talk about and it isn't something that we're educated on.

Karon: Yes, as a society we don't recognise grief when the loss isn't a death. You have had many, many losses in your life starting from your birth. Can you tell us about them?

Louis: My mother, was only 16 when I was born. She found it very challenging and traumatic to be pregnant. She thought about termination. To me as a baby in that situation, I was completely not welcome to life. It still impacts my life, my choices, and my way of being today. What I've learned in my journey so far is that the first few months my mother completely rejected me and then she decided to adopt me out. I was adopted by a woman who desperately wanted a child and moved heaven and earth to adopt me. But when she picked me up, she took one look at me and went, "You're black." I was rejected from the moment she saw me.

I've come to understand **I went through life carrying the unresolved grief of not being welcome, not feeling safe in the world and not feeling I belong.** Even though I couldn't language it until I was in my thirties, it still impacted my relationships and it impacted my ability to succeed in life. I always thought I had to overachieve. I could never be me because that was not enough. I'd be rejected. I became a perfectionist and a control freak. I micromanaged my environment so that I could keep myself safe.

Karon: What you raise is the beliefs that children develop, when they have these losses; beliefs about themselves in the world, and they grow up with them and often don't challenge them. You probably also took on 'I'm not enough', based on what you said.

Louis: 'I'm not safe' became my worldview. As I moved through life, it became 'people aren't safe' and 'the world's not safe'. Those beliefs then shaped my world view and impacted every area of my life. It impacted my relationship with myself. I saw myself through the lens of, I'm not safe, I'm not welcome, I'm not loved. Then I attracted other people who treated me that way, and I accepted that as normal. The first 20 years of my life were quite tumultuous. For a long time, I had asthma, panic attacks and a lot of trouble regulating my breathing, which I now associate with grief, because I would hold my breath, waiting for impact.

My adopted father was a prisoner in a Japanese prison camp. He was traumatised and he was racist against olive skin and dark hair. My family were all English and had fair skin, red hair, and blue eyes. Then I turned up. Years later, one of my brothers said to me, "Oh yeah, mum, was going to leave you there, she tried to leave you there, but she couldn't." Then when I came home, my father, who was a raging alcoholic, decided I was adorable. Then my mother started to hate me because I was my father's favourite. That was not a very welcoming place either. Dad was now an active alcoholic and he'd been kicked out of the house a few times, by the law. He sold everything that wasn't buttoned-down and drank perfume and methylated spirits. He went through a really hard time readjusting to normal life after the prison camp.

They had four sons. One had passed before I came on the scene and the other three had grown up and left. We didn't celebrate Christmas. I came into a home that was almost as isolated as my mother's womb. **Then when I went out into the world, I watched people in shopping centres, children with their mum and dad going shopping to buy shoes for school, having lunch or going to the movies, normal everyday stuff. I would long for that. I didn't realise that longing was grief over the 'loss of the life' I never had, the loss of the parenting I never had, and the loss of a loving family I never got to experience.**

Karon: I think each child recognises that they're entitled to be loved and protected. How do we accommodate that when it doesn't happen? It leaves unresolved grief.

Louis: I believe that our soul is the part that's calling us back to wake up to remember. It's a great learning to wake up and remember, but it's also painful. "Well, hang on a minute, why didn't I have a mum that tucked me into bed every night and read me a story? Or, why didn't I have a father that did that instead of this?" I had a family who would drink and then when they drank enough, they would come looking for me to either sexually, physically or verbally abuse me. It was traumatic. **As an adult I worked through the shame of what had happened, I worked through the anger and the trauma, but I didn't work through the grief. I could never understand why it didn't shift. I'd done a lot of work and thought, why is it still showing up? Then I realised it was the grief over the life I never had.**

Karon: Nobody in your childhood gave you the opportunity to grieve.

Louis: No. **We were never taught to express our feelings. I've never even seen anyone grieve. I wouldn't have even known what it looked like.** If someone had said to me in my childhood, what was the definition of grief, I would have said that it's something you do when someone dies. I still have no idea why in the bardo I thought it would be a good idea to have all these experiences, but it has served me well, now that I've moved out the other end, because now I can be of service to other women that are going through abuse.

Karon: When you talk about the bardo, are you referring to the Buddhist belief in reincarnation? My understanding is the 'bardo' is where our soul goes between lives on earth.

Louis: **It's a soul healing. I believe before my birth I chose my parents and life experiences that would allow my soul to evolve. I believe the soul is eternal and that we have different lifetimes to work through soul lessons.**

Karon: Lou can you tell me about your search for your birthmother?

Louis: I started looking for her, but it's almost impossible because in my day when you were adopted, they doctored all the medical records so you couldn't find your parents. I found a medical certificate snooping through my adopted mother's papers. I knew the hospital where I was born, but it had burned and the records went somewhere else and were lost. I knew I was born in Moree, NSW. The birth certificate had my mother's name and who my father was. I was called 'Unknown Reed'. They didn't even name me.

I started having these dreams that felt like nightmares, where I'm trying to dial a number and the phone was dissolving. It kept disappearing. Over about a year or two, each time I would get one more number. Eventually, I had a full number and I kept getting this, 'You've got to call the number. Call the number.' I thought, 'How stupid. Why would I call the number?' Eventually, I picked up the phone and called and said, "Can I speak to Dorothy Reed, please?" A woman said, "Yes speaking." Well, I almost fell off the chair. I didn't know what to do then. I said, "You went to school with my mother and I'm putting together a birthday party. I wanted to surprise her and try and find some friends from school." She replied, "Oh, honey, I don't think that's me because I'm too old for that." Bursting into tears I said, "I'm sorry for lying to you. I'm trying to find my birthmother. I'm adopted, I know her name's Dorothy Reed and I was born in Moree Hospital on the 3 March in 1963." She replied, "Oh, my God, I'm the nurse that delivered you, I'm not your mother. Your auntie lives next door and your mother's been searching for you all her life. What's your phone number? Give me five minutes. Stay by the phone and I'll get her to call you." She raced next door and told my mother's sister. Moree's a small town and apparently the Reeds owned the hardware store and were well-known. Within five minutes, my mother rings on the phone. "Hello?" That's how I met her.

Karon: Was there an ongoing relationship?

Louis: Oh, we tried. I met her and her best friend who were together when I was conceived in New Zealand. She told me that she was raped. First, the story was she had sex with a guitarist in a band. But then eventually her friend said, "Actually, what really happened was, we were out one night in a club, she had a few drinks and the man probably didn't understand the word 'no'. She was 16 and when we came back here her mother had died." She was 16, in a small country town and that's why she gave me up for adoption. She never had any other children. Her husband was a raging alcoholic. I lost contact. Years later, I tried to find her numerous times, but I've never been able to find her since. She had really, bad endometriosis, which I'm sure I inherited from her.

Karon: I guess we all need to know our history, don't we?

Louis: Give language to it at least. **I felt like I took my power back. I realised that I wasn't thrown away, because for many years I felt like I was rubbish, thrown out with the garbage. Meeting her helped me put things in perspective. She gave me up because she was 16 and didn't know any better, and couldn't look after me, and she was going through her own trauma.**

Karon: I believe you also had a really, traumatic experience in your teens.

Louis: I was kidnapped, tortured and raped by a group of young men and left to die in a creek. I was only 13 or 14. My life was that chaotic at home that no one even noticed I was missing. When I finally made my way home, I was cut from head to toe and had clearly been beaten. I walked in the door and my mother gave me a backhander, called me a slut and sent me to bed. She grounded me and I never got any medical attention. I never got any help, nothing. **Later in life I realised that I had the whole trauma and grief of the loss of innocence of my sexuality. Growing up I never had an opportunity to explore sex in a healthy way with a partner, it was taken away from me.** Then when I did grow up and had sexual relationships with men, it was incredibly painful. It was never a pleasant experience. It was always traumatic. After being raped. I felt that sex was all I had to offer in a relationship which really impacted my relationships. I then stopped having relationships and then had random sex with random people. Sexual abuse at such a young age shaped the way that I moved forward with my sexuality. There was the grief of the loss of sexual innocence, the grief of the great sex life I could have had. I didn't feel whole. I felt like an important piece of me had been taken away. I can't honestly say that I've healed that part. The way that I healed was to become celibate.

Karon: In some ways pushing it aside, it's too hard to deal with?

Louis: I put it in a box. It was too challenging to work with. It was too painful. When I was sexually active, I was having constant operations, and with endometriosis, once the period starts, you can't stop the pain. It impacted my whole life.

Karon: Did it leave you feeling different to other women?

Louis: The only woman in my life was my mother and she was very distant and cold. I guess I took that on board. I certainly didn't have girlfriends to have these kinds of conversations with. It affected my relationship with my feminine. I came to really resent my feminine because it was so damn hard and so painful and who would ever want to be this? Then at some point in my healing journey, it was about learning to welcome my feminine back in as part of the whole, and to heal that wound. I had spent 90% of my life living through my masculine and rejecting the feminine.

Karon: That makes a lot of sense. I can understand that you probably had posttraumatic stress disorder (PTSD) from the rape.

Louis: I've been taught, I did get PTSD, but it was never diagnosed back then and now I'm left with it. I can't stand being touched. It goes through my whole energy system. It's like a feeling of skin-crawling. If there's a sleazy person in the room or on TV, my whole skin crawls. I was also sexually abused as a child in the home. Even now I can still be challenged by that unless I can see people coming and I'm welcoming it. But if someone is sitting next to me and they put their hand on my knee, without me noticing, I'll jump. I still have the hypervigilance of PTSD. Even now, some men, if they sit too close and they go to scratch their head or they lift their arm up, I can find myself thinking, 'Oh shit, they're going to hit me.' It still happens to this day. Sometimes I'm still triggered by a sound or smell. It's quite insidious.

Karon: It's really impacted your whole adult life, hasn't it?

Louis: Without a doubt, even today. I have a male dog as a step towards feeling comfortable with male energy in the house. For many years I lived in high rises with security doors and security systems, I'd kept myself small and contained. **When you have a trauma on a deep soul**

level like that, it impacts you in every area and you don't even realise you have it unless you pause and do the work.

Karon: Can you explain being so successful in your career while being so traumatised in your personal life?

Louis: I found that I was so sensitive to the people in my environment. When I was young and my father hit the letterbox as he was coming in, I knew exactly who I had to be to survive the night. I was a kid and I could feel who was coming in, mum, dad, my brother. I could feel their energy before they even came in the door. That meant I was really attuned to other people and I fell into sales. I knew what people needed before they knew what they needed, and I was incredibly successful. I was good at adapting to be whoever people needed me to be. It wasn't a conscious manipulation. It was a subconscious manipulation to keep me safe. I'd put on this mask and I'd walk out the door and I'd look like I was the life of the party, an extrovert and confident. In reality, I was an introvert. I'd come home and I'd be so exhausted from having to play this part in the world that I ended up with adrenal chronic fatigue. It started with a fall up a step when I was going to an office for a meeting. That accident left me with long term chronic pain which led to chronic fatigue. But in fact, what I've learned is that my system learned to default to PTSD or trauma from the womb. My mother was in trauma because she was raped and I was born with PTSD, with trauma. My mental, emotional, physical, and spiritual all learned trauma as the default. I was constantly creating this chaotic external environment. It's the only environment I knew how to survive in. I knew how to fight back, I knew how to push, I knew how to control my environment. When I started doing spiritual work and started to experience peace, I started having panic attacks because I didn't know how to be inside of joy.

Karon: When you say you started doing work, do you mean emotional healing work on yourself?

Louis: Yes, that was emotional and physical healing work.

Karon: What led you to that?

Louis: **I was drinking, I was an alcoholic and I found that the alcohol**

helped numb the emotions, because any emotion was too much even if I had a great day. If you think of it as I had a glass ceiling that kept me safe and well, I numbed underneath that. Whether I had a terrible experience or a great experience, anything that took my emotions over that glass ceiling I couldn't manage. I didn't know how to be inside of that. Because from a very young age, the way I coped was to numb. I started with alcohol, food, money, sex. One day, I'll never forget it. For the very first time, I woke up and I was too sick to drink, but I was too sick not to drink because my life hadn't changed. My body said, we can't do this anymore. I was terrified. The healing journey started there. I kept getting alcoholic poisoning every time I drank. That was a scary moment because alcohol had always been the solution, and had been my family. Whenever I was lonely or whenever a feeling came up, I had Jack, me and Jack Daniels, my bestie, and we would drink. I wouldn't drink outside with people, I needed to be left alone to drink in the way that I needed to drink, which was basically drinking to oblivion. I was completely isolated.

Karon: Was it at that point that you sought help?

Louis: Yes. I walked into a doctor's surgery and he picked me as an alcoholic in one. I was looking for a magic pill that you take for ten days and you're better. He said, well, I'll give you pills for a week, but you need to ring this lady because she can help you. I went back in a week and hadn't rung the lady and he said, "Okay, so I'll give you one more week of pills, but you need to go to an AA meeting every day and you need to ring this lady and you need to have met her before next week." I said, "Why do I want to go to AA?" I had no clue that I was an alcoholic. I was still functioning at that stage. I looked good, I had a beautiful home, and a beautiful business. Everything on the outside looked good. I went to a meeting every day and had the card signed because I wanted the pills. I remember when I was invited to share, they said, "Tell us a bit about yourself and why you're here." I replied, "Oh, I'm not an alcoholic. I'm only here because the doctor said if I come every day, he'll give me a prescription." They went, "Oh, okay, great, welcome anyway." They were all alcoholics and got it. Then I met this lady a few times and I would go back every week and the doctor would give me another week's pills so that I kept doing these meetings. Then I realised,

'Oh gee, maybe I have got something in common with these people, but I don't think I'm an alcoholic.'

That's when I knew for the first time that I was an alcoholic and I did have a problem. I couldn't do life anymore. I needed to be locked away and I needed someone to take care of me. I signed myself into rehabilitation for a year, packed everything up, gave everything away, sorted everything out and checked in. I'm still not sure I thought I was an alcoholic, but life was too hard. I went in and started getting well, that was the beginning of my journey to wellness. But we never talked about grief. I didn't know that I was grieving for the life I never had, grieving for the family I never had and grieving for the relationship with myself that I never had. I didn't understand. Grief was not a word in my vocabulary at that time. That was when the grief started to come up, but it was so deep underneath everything else that it was still hidden for a very long time.

Karon: I guess when you stopped drinking, feelings started surfacing.

Louis: They did. In rehabilitation they teach you about feelings, they had this chart with all these faces on them. Then you'd have to try and language your feelings, e.g. I'm sad today, I'm angry today, I'm whatever today. Then the counsellors would constantly say, how are you today? They wouldn't allow us to say fine; "No, use your faces." I was learning how to live in a community in a healthy way. We all had duties that we had to do each day. Teaching me to be responsible, to care for myself, to engage with others, we'd have a communal meal room and how to sit at a table and not argue and fight or walk off. It was very clever the way they structured it. Then we would have teaching modules, and go to counselling each day. It was helping us to find that new structure that would help us when we left rehab and went back out into the world.

Karon: What happened when you went back into the world?

Louis: It was a big transition because I'd been in there for a year. There is a halfway house, to help you transition, and it was right next to my homegroup. I had to go to meetings every day and learn how to pay bills; I had to learn how to shop, cook, that kind of thing. I started working with my sponsor. Every weekend we would get together like a family.

We'd go out for dinner and a meeting. I learned how to meet people, mix and be out in the world and not drink. It was a real process. It wasn't simple.

Karon: It sounds like it took some years.

Louis: It took about six years. I had an incredible sponsorship who took me through the 36 principles, which are the 12 steps, 12 traditions, and 12 concepts. That was incredible. I had a great life and I loved it. But then it was time to leave and step out of AA and do something different. Grief is kind of a funny thing because I realised, I was grieving the life I never had, the community I never had, and as my life started to expand, there were more layers of grief. I didn't know that it was beneficial to have a community of people and friends. Then as I started stepping out and expanding, I would get two things. One, I had grief over why it had been so long, and two, the childhood I didn't have.

Karon: Did you allow the grief to come to the surface?

Louis: Well, I have to say, until I met you, I didn't know it was grief. I kept thinking it was a longing. The language that I would use is, I was aware the longing would come to the surface and then the anger would kick in. I obviously wasn't resourced enough to name it as grief. But as soon as we did the grief workshop with you the first time, I could see all the pieces linking together and going, oh my God, that was grief and that's grief and that's grief and that's grief. That's why the trauma hadn't shifted because I've worked on everything but grief.

Karon: Well, somehow, you've moved from such a traumatic childhood and early adulthood to where you are today, which is the founder of Integrative Medicine Institute. Do you want to talk about that and how that all came about?

Louis: I wanted to help women get to a place where they're ready to reach out and ask for help because most people know they're in trauma, but they're not ready to do anything about it. My intention was to give them information and then show them how they could practically apply it in their life. Integrative Medicine Institute started from a book for sharing my story and evolved into an online training campus where you could come in and you're aware you have trauma and you can start to language it and get to a place where you may want help at some point. Then when you're ready you can come and deep dive with other women. I really saw the value of community in my story and I wanted to create a safe place where women could gather and share and then go out and help others. **I don't know if I would have been able to be of service at such a deep soul level without my trauma. I do believe that was part of it. I unpacked the steps I took to move through my trauma journey.**

Karon: It's fabulous that something so wonderful has come out of your trauma, **but I do wonder about forgiveness because you must surely have felt very unforgiving towards all the people who've abused you throughout your life.**

Louis: For a long time, I did. I was very angry at my mother the most. I remember making amends. That was something that my mentor invited me to do even though my mother treated me poorly. I took that on as my way of being and I treated her poorly. We were at loggerheads every time we caught up. I perpetuated it and I allowed it to be a way of being, although I didn't make the choice that it was my way of being. **But not making a choice is making a choice. Therefore, unconsciously I chose to be an angry person.**

I had this amazing life in Singapore when my mother became very unwell. My father had died not long before, the last thing he said to me was, "Take care of your mother. Promise me." I said, "Yes, I promise." My brother called me and said, we're going to have to put her into a home. I know that mum and dad didn't want that. I said, "I'll move back, and I'll look after her." My brother almost fell off the chair. I almost vomited when I said it out loud.

Before she passed, I made amends and said, "I'm sorry for my part. I'm mindful that I've been very angry towards you and I apologise." She didn't know what to do or what to say, and that was okay. I've learned that making amends is not about the other person accepting me or loving me. It's about me clearing my energy. I said to my mother, "Is there anything that you'd like to say to me? I'm happy to hear anything if you feel I've hurt you and I haven't made amends for that? I'm here and I'm happy to talk about it."

I remember ringing my mentor at the time and I was a bit shellshocked, but for a very long time after that, I had an identity crisis. The amends worked and I'd let go of all the anger. **The anger at her was what was helping me move through life. It was almost my energy source. I then had to start reshaping who am I now, when I'm not an angry person, how do I engage with her? How do I engage with others? It was a process. It wasn't simple and it wasn't comfortable, but it was a great thing to do.** When she died, we were in a loving relationship, as best as we could be. She died and I felt at peace that I'd said everything I needed to say. She'd said everything she needed to say, our karma was complete.

Karon: Do you have any advice for other people who need to find forgiveness for others about how to go about it?

Louis: **I believe we all agreed to play certain parts and certain roles so that we could have experiences that would allow us to grow and expand.** For me, this is the school where I'm learning about sexuality, masculine and feminine health. I believe that those people who I have come across in this lifetime have also had an agreement to share certain experiences. Whether I'm the one giving you the experience or you're the one giving me the experience, we're doing it from a place of love, to help our soul evolve. That is how I came to a place of forgiveness. After making amends to my mother and seeing the difference that made in my life, in my internal and external world, I've not had another operation.

Karon: Wow. Isn't that interesting? I've heard it said that lack of forgiveness causes dis-ease in our life.

Louis: I've worked with the energy long enough to see that everything is synchronistic. **There is no chaos. There is no random. There is a gift in everything that happens.** It's more about being awake to our life and what's unfolding in the moment. **We have experiences, they shape our beliefs, our beliefs shape our worldview, the worldview is reflected in our body. When we have disease and sickness, it comes from our thinking.**

Karon: That's interesting. This is awesome work you're doing.

Louis: Well, it's my passion. I love it. Whilst I still have chronic fatigue, I'm always able to show up fully. **I love being able to help women go out and help other women.**

Karon: Is there anything else that you felt you wanted to say?

Louis: **After my accident there was a lot of grief around the life I lost**, even though I can now see that it was a self-correction. I fell up a couple of steps and I had injuries and chronic pain for 22 months. That led to adrenal chronic fatigue. I've never had anything so debilitating physically. I was always able to push through. But this really made me stop. They called it an adjustment disorder and I started seeing a psychologist, but I needed to grieve the loss of the life that I had. Before the accident I was able to go to work, function, travel, meet clients, go out for dinner and do amazing things. Suddenly it stopped. I could barely get out of bed for months. I couldn't feed myself. I couldn't dress myself. It was a real shock to the system. Recovering from that was a long journey because, in my head, I could always see myself as this other person.

I guess this is the first time I had, other than the sexual abuse, a significant loss event. I was grieving the loss of my life as a corporate high flyer. I had a beautiful sports car, a beautiful apartment in Bondi, Sydney. Flying all over the world. I had a certain income that allowed me to live that way. Then suddenly, I had this accident and it all stopped. **I didn't realise it was grief. I kept thinking it was a longing and I pushed myself so hard to get back to this certain place in time, the day before my accident where I thought my life was perfect. I needed to grieve losing that lifestyle.**

Karon: **The grief journey is all about adjusting. It's about learning who you are in the world without this thing or person that you've lost and adjusting your life accordingly.**

Louis: The big adjustment was learning to drive with the driving aid, learning to get dressed and not being able to use my right arm. I had been isolated for so long in that 22 months that I wasn't even able to go to the letterbox. I had agoraphobia; I couldn't even sit in a cafe. I was at a point in my life where everything had been stripped away, like the alcoholism.

I had to relearn life again. But it turned out to be a blessing because now I'm doing my sacred work and I now have a healthy relationship with myself, with friends, with the community: It was a course correct.

Karon: It sounds like if you hadn't had the accident you wouldn't be where you are today.

Louis: No, I'm confident of that. I would not have stopped and done the deep work that I needed to do. I needed excruciating amounts of pain to change.

Karon: Is that because you'd learned to soldier on through everything.

Louis: You take it. I was sexually abused one night. Next morning, everyone else was acting like nothing had happened. Denial was the way forward. You get up and keep moving on. Denial is not a way forward, it's a great way to cope during short periods of time. And that's what I love about your work, you're not saying don't grieve, you're saying, here are the natural steps to move through grief. This is what it looks like in less than optimal. This is what it looks like optimal. I love the work that you're doing. It's amazing.

Karon: Thank you Lou. Can I ask you, were there points in your journey where you asked, "Why me?"

Louis: **Most of my life my mantra was, 'I'm too broken'. I felt I was too broken to ever heal or to even live.** I remember the night before they checked me out of rehabilitation, I lay there paralysed with fear. I thought, 'How the fuck am I going to do this? How do I do life?' I had no life skills, none. For a very long time I was terrified, and anger was my motivation. Anger kept me moving. When I checked out of rehab, I had to get a sponsor or a homegroup. I thankfully got a great sponsor and she would say to me, "so what's your plan when you check out?" I was checking out to commit suicide. She encouraged me to do the AA steps with her. There's a lot of reasons why I left, but I went every day for six years. I'm grateful now for that experience because I can connect in with people at that level. Their soul can hear me because they know that I've truly experienced it and I've moved through it and I've come out the other end. I'm living proof that there is life after trauma, that we can live a full life.

Karon: It's such a gift to be able to sit with people and hear their pain so they can begin to heal. Lou, it's been fascinating listening to you. I am so grateful for your willingness to share your life with such honesty and openness.

Lou: I'm happy to be of service to people. I'm grateful I can be a part of this exciting venture that you're moving forward with. Congratulations.

Key Concepts

Abused children often find themselves on a path of self-destruction that can lead to choosing drugs and/or alcohol to cope with their feelings and then joining the ranks of the homeless as they escape their abusive home environment. It's a terrible downward spiral towards a life of misery. However, with good intervention by responsible, supportive adults they can go down the path of finding work, a career and live a healthy adult life. Unfortunately for Louis this did not happen. But she found a way out with a lot of good support from AA.

Buddhists believe death is a natural part of the life cycle and leads to rebirth. This belief in reincarnation – that a person's spirit remains close by and seeks out a new body and new life – is a comforting and important principle of Buddhism. These beliefs have helped Louis to find meaning in her traumatic life.

PTSD is a disorder which results from experiencing or observing a traumatic event. It can last months or years, with triggers that can bring back memories of the trauma accompanied by intense emotional and physical reactions. Symptoms may include nightmares or flashbacks, avoidance of situations that bring back the trauma, heightened reactivity to stimuli, anxiety or depressed mood.

Treatment includes different types of psychotherapy as well as medications to manage symptoms.

Things that helped Louis's recovery:

1. Seeking a doctor to help her and following the doctor's advice.

2. Recognising and acknowledging she was an alcoholic.

3. Admitting herself to rehabilitation realising she could not stop drinking without assistance and support 24 hours a day.

4. Attending Alcoholic Anonymous (AA) meetings daily for six years and doing the AA steps.

5. Finding forgiveness for her mother and others who had wronged her and letting go of her anger.

6. Seeking psychological support to work through her wounds from her traumatic life.

7. Finding spiritual beliefs that supported her.

8. Recognising her grief for what it was over the many losses she experienced and doing the grief work.

9. Creating meaning from her experiences by using it to be of service to other women, through her work and creating Integrative Medicine Institute as a legacy of her traumatic life.

Chapter 4

Karen Sydnè-Scott

---

*"I am thankful for all of those who said no to me.
It's because of them I'm doing it myself."*

Albert Einstein

KAREN Sydnè-Scott Biography

Karen is an International Bestselling Author, Speaker, High Performance Coach, Clinical Hypnotherapist and Entrepreneur. She is recognised as a leading specialist in the area of Business, Success, Wealth Creation, Self-Development and Psychological Transformation.

She became an entrepreneur at a young age and started her first business at 18 years old. For the past two decades Karen has owned and operated over 16 successful businesses and worked, travelled, consulted and spoken to hundreds of people in several countries teaching her secrets to wealth, success and life leadership skills.

In 2011 Karen's life changed when she was buried underneath a two-storey building in the Christchurch, New Zealand, earthquake and survived!!! She lost everything that she had worked so hard for over many years.

In true entrepreneur spirit Karen rose from the rubble to create success once again, her mental toughness, courage, leadership and inspiration has led her to continue to grow, rebuild and now help others around the world.

Karen for the past ten years has worked, shared the stage with and trained with other inspiring world leaders such as Anthony Robbins, Darren Stephens, Pat Mesiti and Allan Pease, just to name a few.

She is the author of international bestselling book *Rising From the Rubble* and also co-authored *Pardon Me, I'm Prospering!* and *The Secret Diaries of Inspirational Women*. Karen contributes articles to many magazines. Karen is highly qualified and certified in various fields; Neuro-Linguistic Programming, Master of Hypnosis, High Performance Coaching, International Author/Speaker.

karensydnecoaching@gmail.com

www.karensydne.com

The Interview

Karon: Karen, in your fascinating book, *Rising from The Rubble*, you mentioned you developed polio from a vaccination at 18 months. Can you tell us what happened to you and how that affected your childhood?

Karen: Instead of giving me protection from contracting polio, it gave me the virus and I was left unable to walk. Apparently, in those days it was a live vaccine. My mother said by the time we got home I took a seizure. My parents noticed I was dragging my leg and couldn't get up onto the couch. They took me to the hospital. The doctors thought I had meningitis. They did a lumbar puncture test and the results showed I had polio. I couldn't walk. The doctor's said I would never walk again. Lucky for me my dad disagreed and said leaving me lying in the cot with no movement or exercise I wouldn't walk again, but with exercise, I would. Against the doctor's advice he signed me out of hospital into his care. Mum told me that Dad got a doll's pram and he had me holding onto it. He walked me round and round the room on his hands and knees for months and months and months till he finally got me to walk again. So that story has been a real driving force in my life. From that, I had always thought, whatever is to be, if it's going to be, it is up to me. If dad hadn't done that, I may never have walked.

I've always had positive thinking. I can remember sitting on the hospital bed, and I can still picture the doctors in their white coats. The doctors continued to disagree with my parents saying even though I was walking then it wouldn't last. I would deteriorate and end up in a wheelchair for the rest of my life. I can remember thinking, "Who's he talking about? That won't be me." Over the years, I did absolutely everything to not let that be my outcome. I did have lots of surgeries and I wore callipers on my leg and was a crippled child. I was bullied at school and pushed over all the time. I learned coping strategies to help myself. In my first week at school when I was pushed over, the only thing that I could find to stand up for myself was to throw stones at the kids, which was an absolute no-no. I was the one stood in front of the class and given the strap, not the ones pushing me over.

Karon: Oh, that's terrible, isn't it?

Karen: Yeah. But it most definitely helped shape me into who I am. I have lived all my life in constant pain and endless surgeries, it all became second nature to me. I have coping strategies to deal with the pain, because every step in my life has been painful. I've taken that belief that each step is leading me to greatness, and I've got to keep going. I'm well-known for every business I've had. Every car I've had is filled with shoes. Under my desk was always shoes. And that's how I'd keep going. I would change my shoes every hour of the day, have a different height and a different style to try and relieve the pain.

Karon: No wheelchair?

Karen: No wheelchair. Never had a wheelchair.

Karon: You can walk around quite satisfactorily now, can you? What an awesome story.

Karen: It's probably 20 years ago, as surgery had advanced, I had my right leg lengthened. I could now put my right heel and my foot on the ground for the first time in my life. Walking was much better. **I had to learn to walk in my head by talking to myself and that is where I learned that the mind is so powerful.** As I was walking towards people, I would be talking to myself in my head all the time, saying, "Don't limp. Don't fall over. Walk straight. Keep your feet one step in front of the other." That self-talk enabled me to walk better. It became second nature. I've had a lot of cafes and restaurants and when I'd be carrying plates with food to people, I'd certainly be making sure that I didn't fall over.

Karon: I think most people know Christchurch, New Zealand, was hit by a series of devastating earthquakes starting on the 4 September 2011. Where were you on that day?

Karen: I think it was about 3.50 am and I was in bed asleep. I'd never experienced an earthquake like that in my life. With the earthquakes I'd previously experienced I would think, "Oh, was that an earthquake?" I'd be looking around to see if there was a light swinging or something. That night, I woke to… well, it was horrendous, the noise and the shaking and all my dishes flying out of the cupboards, smashing on the ground. It was frightening. I didn't know what was happening. I've never forgotten it, it reminded me of a war zone like movies you've seen on TV, because it was continual helicopters and police sirens. The sirens were never-ending. Christchurch had never been a place that had been predicted to have earthquakes. Wellington was. The next day, I couldn't get into the city near my business and I didn't have any food in my house because I used to eat all my meals at work. There was no electricity and it was freezing cold. I was stuck and I couldn't get anywhere until they had the army come in and the police allowed me into the city.

Karon: It must have been terrifying.

Karen: It was scary being all by myself.

Karon: Can you tell me a bit about the cafe business that you had in Christchurch at the time?

Karen: It was a cafe bar right in Christchurch CBD. Christchurch had a lot of old brick buildings. The building my business was in and the one next door were brick buildings. When I returned, the buildings in the street were heavily destroyed and there were bricks everywhere. However, the cafe where my business was had been earthquake-strengthened with heaps of metal beams in the walls and roof. It took two or three weeks before we were allowed back in the business and it was hard for the next six months because people were fearful to come into the city. The street my business was in was cordoned off. Cars weren't allowed to drive down it. There was scaffolding everywhere. It was a very hard six months of trading, as the council weren't giving discounts off anything, rents, rates, nothing. We even had to pay for having tables and chairs on the street when you couldn't even have your tables and chairs on the street because of all the scaffolding. It was very tough times.

Every day, every night, we would have earthquakes. The earthquakes would swing the fridge doors open and all the bottles would crash out onto the ground for that six months. As soon as we felt one coming, my daughter and I would run to a fridge and hold onto the doors. Each night, I would put the tables and chairs up against them so they couldn't open. Everybody was very stressed and tired because there wasn't a night in that six months that you didn't have aftershocks. The aftershocks were still bigger than any earthquake that I had previously experienced. They were frightening and I'd think that it was going to be as bad as that first night.

Because people say this only happens to you once in lifetime, I would reassure myself thinking, 'Okay, you have had your big earthquake, you have got to get on and get this right' because I've experienced it and it's okay. But then another huge earthquake happened on the 22 February 2011 at about 12.50 pm. It was lucky, because the 12:00 lunch people had gone, and the 1:00 pm people hadn't come in. There were only a handful of customers in there at the time. They were down by the door and able to get out.

When it hit, I knew that it was different than anything I'd experienced before. It was so loud and so violent. People have said, if you haven't experienced it, you wouldn't believe that it could happen. The big one-litre spirit bottles, which are heavy, were on the shelf and they didn't fall over they were lifting up off the shelves, and shooting through the air like torpedoes. **My daughter was standing beside me. I said to her, "Quick, we've got to get out." She couldn't move. She was frozen. I grabbed her and we moved. We only had time to take about four steps. It was like the roof opened up and there was a big avalanche of bricks and rubble coming down on us. We were buried in seconds. There was no way we could get out or move.**

Karon: Were you still conscious?

Karen: I remember we were down on the concrete ground and we couldn't move with all the bricks and rubble on top of us. They would have been as high as the ceiling. My lungs were filled with lots of dust and mortar. It was like someone opened up the roof, and poured all these bricks and rubble onto us. I couldn't understand what had happened at the time. Afterwards I learned it was the building next door to us, because I couldn't figure where it had all come from as we didn't have another storey above us. The next door, three-storey brick building, had four layers of bricks in each wall. It had collapsed and that's what tumbled through the roof, lots and lots of bricks.

Karon: Were you and your daughter beside each other face down?

Karen: I wasn't aware where she was, but we were close together. I don't really remember much about it. **I know I didn't want my daughter to die. I was very fearful, I believed we were going to die. I didn't see how we were going to get out.**

Karon: Because you couldn't help yourself?

Karen: No. Looking back, I don't remember anything other than that. From my time being buried, that's all I could remember about it. This was where I was going to die. I can remember someone saying, "Is there anybody in there?" I must have yelled out because I remember someone saying to me, "I can see your hands, but you have to stretch out so I can reach you." I couldn't believe that someone was really saying that. That this could be real. That someone was there. It felt very surreal. They kept saying, "Come on, stretch your hands out. Stretch your hands out and we can get you." I remember really trying, and my clothes were stuck on something so I couldn't get my arm free. Then I must have ripped it and then I felt someone touching my fingertips.

If we'd taken one more step, that metal beam would have… we would have been dead. But somehow, that metal beam had kept enough up underneath all the rubble that they could pull us out. One minute it was lunchtime, and then it was night-time. I didn't know what had happened in between other than we were trapped. Then we had to try and get ourselves home. There was no one to help you. When we got out, it was still scary.

Karon: There wasn't an ambulance to take you to hospital?

Karen: No, everything was too busy. There were 186 people killed. There were no services available to help us. The sight was unbelievable. Someone was killed in a car right outside where we were and another one in the shop down the street. It was absolute bedlam. We had to walk and try and get to my daughter's car. We couldn't get through the city, so we had to go this long way out of the city.

Karon: Was she uninjured? Could you both walk?

Karen: Well we had to.

Karon: And you weren't aware of what had happened in terms of your injuries?

Karen: No, we knew that we had to try and get out of it. I'd lost everything in the earthquake, like my bag, phone and laptop. I didn't have anything.

We had a scary drive over big, big mountains of dirt and rubble. We would be sliding off onto the other side and there was water running everywhere. It was extremely scary. My daughter was very stressed, very agitated and upset. She didn't know what had happened to her children and she was wanting to get home. She lives out of Christchurch. Her kids were primary school aged and they were at home. They didn't know where she was. Her husband was working away from home and wasn't anywhere near Christchurch.

Karon: I think, any parent's first thoughts are for their children and if they are safe and alive. Like you with her. You wanted her to live.

Karen: I was probably in shock and very shaken, but I was too ill to notice. I had massive headaches. I couldn't get to the hospital immediately and didn't have scans. When they ended up doing the x-rays, they read the x-ray wrong and I should have been in a neck brace. There were no services. Everything was shut down. No ATM machines, no petrol in Christchurch no supermarkets open. It was like there was nothing. My other family from Marlborough, (which is four hours' drive from Christchurch) ended up coming down and getting us. On the way back, we ran out of petrol and had to get a farmer to give us petrol to get home.

Karon: It sounds like everything was a struggle.

Karen: It was a huge time. I went back to falling over and not being able to walk properly because of my fractured skull, spine and head injuries. I could no longer concentrate. It was too painful. I suffered migraines and I'd be vomiting every day. My short-term memory was very, very bad. I couldn't concentrate.

In the six months between the earthquakes, I kept having these visions of being buried beneath the building. I actually saw what had happened to me, but I didn't tell anybody, because I thought they'd be thinking, 'You're nuts. Nothing happened to you.' Every night, I would prepare myself, and I'd always have my phone charged and I'd have my car keys in my bag. I'd have my handbag all packed every night with everything so I was ready to get out the door and into my car and I didn't have to look for anything. I did that even at work. That day was too fast and there was no way I could get to anything. The morning of the earthquake, when I pulled up and parked my car, I heard a little voice in my head that said, 'Don't park your car there. That building will fall on your car.' That's something that's vivid to me, and I stopped only for a split second. I was peering down out of my driver's door at this big tall building. And then that logical side came in, and because I didn't believe there was going to be another earthquake, I said to myself, 'Don't be so goddamned stupid. Get to work. There's not going to be another earthquake.' I left my car there and that building fell on my car.

Karon: Wow. So, you didn't trust those inner instincts.

Karen: Not then, because I hadn't…

Karon: I bet you do now.

Karen: Yes. Because I hadn't had them before, and I thought 'Oh, that's stupid.' I didn't take any notice of it. I certainly do now. Anything that I haven't listened to, which sometimes I don't, has always happened. It might be something simple like, 'Shift that plate, because you'll knock it over.' If I don't the next thing, it smashes to the floor. I laugh about it now. I'm like, 'Oh, my god. You knew that was going to happen.' I really do take notice now, because I know that it's true and it was so dramatic that day that I can't forget it. I've never told many people that, because people don't believe that stuff. My car was flattened with that building. If I'd moved my car it would have been all right. Why did that get said to me on that day and not any other day in that six months?

My daughter doesn't recall anything, and she won't talk about it. I can't ask her a thing about the earthquake. She used to get angry if anybody asked her anything. I've always thought that it would be harder for her being that way and one day she'd talk about it. She says, "I don't know what happened. Someone must have moved me. I don't know how I got where I got."

Karon: That's her way of dealing with it.

Karen: Yes, it is. It was very hard. It was stuff we hadn't dealt with before. It was my decision not to go back to Christchurch, because it was too hard, because I couldn't get anything sorted out. **I couldn't get any insurance. I fought the insurance companies for years. I couldn't get my money. I had no income. My money was gone. I couldn't get my insurance money for my lost property and business or my car. The insurance wouldn't pay out on my car till they had a car to look at. The city was all fenced off, so I couldn't get towed out of the city for months and until it went to the wreckers, they wouldn't pay out. Where I lived was a new apartment I bought in a commercial block. The insurers wouldn't pay out for that either.**

Karon: You'd lost your home as well? [shocked]

Karen: It was badly damaged and needed repairs and apparently, there's an indemnity clause in insurance policies that if it exceeds the insured value, they can choose to pay out the smallest amount they want to, which they tried. They have been extremely difficult to deal with. **Trying to deal with all these people from the insurance company added huge stress and was very challenging** when I had all the headaches. **You can't move forward, because you can't even get your insurance money.** I did the right thing, but they wouldn't pay out.

Karon: Wow. You had no income. No home. No business and no car?

Karen: It was difficult. To this day, that's what frightens me more about an earthquake. It's not the actual earthquake. I'm sure I wouldn't like to be in another big one. But it's the aftermath, what you know you have to deal with, and the years of your life that you have to deal with this stuff afterwards. It's how it challenges you mentally, emotionally and financially. That is the scariest part to me. I wouldn't want to have to go through all that again. **I did decide very quickly that I had to help myself.**

I had two choices. I had two paths I could take. I could stay looking down this path of being the victim and I've lost everything that I had worked for all my life. I had been mortgage-free before the earthquake. I looked at it and thought, 'Okay, I can concentrate on my losses, but there's absolutely nothing I can do to change that. Like, this was an earthquake. It's not something someone did to me. It is nature. It's something that's happened, and there's not a thing that I could do to change it. **I can choose that path, or I can choose, I'm going to help myself and I'm going to do something about that.'** It might have been a month or so that I quite quickly decided I had to do something about my situation. I had no income. I had nothing. I was living with my daughter.

I decided I had to get income. I had always done all the baking at my cafes, so I immediately started baking from home about a month after the earthquake. When I bake, I am in my happy place, so I started this business sending out gift baskets of baking to people. It was called Maggie Jane Homemade Baking after my grandmothers. I went to businesswomen's networking groups and found healing took place there as I shared my experience and found support and encouragement in getting up and going again. I was still experiencing difficulty seeing, and a terrible memory, but with my daughter's support I started getting income again. I went on to start other businesses. I loved that challenge of setting up a business and building it up to a sellable. I wanted to do something new and I started looking into seminars. I was at one about writing a book and I thought 'Oh, my god. This is it.' All the way flying home, I couldn't think of anything else.

I came up with the idea I was going to interview all these people that had been through adversities until they had been able to take those challenges and do something with their life. **Something to help other people who were struggling. It was very hard for people in Christchurch. I wanted to have a book that would motivate people.** It certainly took me a long time. It cost me a lot of interest on credit cards. I had no choice. If I wanted to get going again, I had to have that debt, because I wouldn't have been able to get a loan from the bank, because I had no property.

Karon: No assets?

Karen: It was difficult for years, because no one would lend to me. It was a matter of working. It was probably when people were hearing what I'd been through, and I was asked to do some public talks. It started with things like Rotary and Lions Clubs. And then I started doing my coaching, helping people to grow their businesses.

You've got to make decisions and take action. I think you learn all that from these experiences of loss, grief, challenges and if you decide not to be a victim. You've got to be prepared to change with life.

Life is too short. There is nothing other than death that we don't have some control over. To me, that's what grief is. The real grief is in death. I've lost my father, my brother, and a sister. You can't change that.

Karon: What did you learn about yourself through all these experiences?

Karen: I think it goes back to those early days when I always had challenges with the pain and not walking correctly. I always had that thought from my father, if it was going to be, it was up to me. My attitude was always, 'Well, I'll do it myself.' I haven't relied on other people. **Don't say, "What can someone else do to help me?" I've always said, "Well, what can I do about it?"** You've got to have a vision and to look to the future and not concentrate on the problems you've got. **You've got to take responsibility for your own life.**

Karon: Did you get another home?

Karen: Yes. I've been building and selling in the last few years and trying to make up some money to get myself back into that mortgage-free state again.

Karon: Where do you live now?

Karen: I live in Blenheim, in Marlborough, which is the top of the South Island. But I do work and go to Christchurch often. My daughter still lives there. Unfortunately, we did experience, of late, earthquakes in Marlborough.

Karon: What happens inside of you when there's another earthquake?

Karen: Before the earthquakes, I was never claustrophobic, but I am now, and I wouldn't like that trapped feeling again. I had an MRI scan. They didn't tell me that they would strap my head down and put me right inside the machine. That wasn't long after the earthquake. I wanted to vomit. I wanted to get out but was tied down to this bed. I had to fight that panic. When I drove home afterwards, I had to keep stopping because I was crying all the way home. I didn't realise that it would affect me like that.

It was probably a couple years ago when we had the first big earthquake in Blenheim. The next day, everything was still operating. But on the night, it did bring it back to me, because I did have to hold onto the door frame. It was a huge shake, and everything was crashing out of my kitchen cupboards again. It reminded me of Christchurch. I was fearful that my new house was going to be damaged and I would have to do all this again. Other than that, I never think about earthquakes because you don't know when they're going to happen. There's no warning.

I like to look to the people that have been through huge adversities, much worse than what's ever happened to me. **You've got to have resilience, strength and learn coping skills. I think it's important throughout your life you accept responsibility and deal with the minor things to develop resilience, because even as children, we have challenges.** If your parents or someone else steps in and helps you all the time, you never learn to deal with those things. I think it's always easier if you find someone else to help too. I looked to the people who were worse off than me in the earthquakes. My book was written to help them.

Key Concepts

Catastrophic events like a major earthquake has a long-lasting impact on the people who live through them. While the initial shock and confusion of the disaster soon subsides, for some people feelings of stress, grief, anger and frustration will continue for several years and can be complicated by fighting insurance companies for a payout. As in Karen's case she was left homeless with no car and no income but was not supported by the insurance company she had invested in. This can complicate recovery enormously as it exacerbates the anger and frustration, prevents rebuilding and moving forward in life. Karen's decision to take ownership of her life was a decisive turning point.

People often migrate, either temporarily or permanently, away from a disaster zone to avoid another experience, but they take the feelings and challenges of recovery with them.

Things that helped Karen's recovery:

1. She did not let the earthquake define her. Nor did she let it take away her choices, determination and strength.

2. Karen counted her blessings and felt grateful all her family were still alive.

3. Karen decided very quickly that she had to help herself, realising she didn't want to adopt a victim mentality.

4. Being prepared to change with life, rolling with the punches.

5. Believing she had to take responsibility for her own life and realising we do have a choice in everything.

6. Following the earthquake Karen reflected on all the things that are important to her in her life, her family; her values, beliefs, strengths. Following this review, she made a conscious decision to follow her dreams.

7. She believes in herself and her ability to create income earning businesses.

8. Knowing she is resilient and can survive any event life throws at her.

9. Seeking support through a women's networking group.

10. Helping others was part of her healing process.

11. Her legacy was her book written to help other people who experienced the devastating effects of the earthquakes. The intent was for the reader to feel motivated and inspired to believe their life is in their control.

The front of Ja Basco's where Karen was crushed.

Karen standing to the left of all that remains of the two-storey building under which she was crushed.

> *When my son died the real world collapsed around me and I entered a strange unreal world that seemed to be spinning at great velocity. I was so fragile I was sure I would shatter into a million shards. I disappeared off this planet, only my body remained here.*

Karon Coombs

Chapter 5

Senator the Hon Kristina Keneally

"It is under the greatest adversity that there exists the greatest potential for doing good, both for oneself and others"

The 14th Dalai Lama

KRISTINA KENEALLY Biography

Senator the Hon Kristina Keneally

Born to an Australian mother and an American father, Kristina grew up in the United States, where she completed her secondary and tertiary education.

Kristina moved permanently to Australia in 1994. She joined the Australian Labor Party in 2000. A Member of the Parliament of New South Wales from 2003–12, Kristina was the 42nd Premier of New South Wales (2009–11) and the first woman to hold the office.

An avid basketball player in her youth, Kristina served as the CEO of Basketball Australia from 2012–14, before joining Sky News Australia where she co-hosted the daily lunchtime show To the Point.

In February 2018 Kristina was endorsed by the ALP and elected by the NSW Parliament to fill a casual vacancy in the Australian Senate. She was subsequently appointed Deputy Labor Leader in the Senate, Shadow Minister for Home Affairs and the Shadow Minister for Immigration and Citizenship by Labor Leader Anthony Albanese in June 2019.

Ms. Keneally has served on a range of benevolent boards and charities including her role as the Chairperson of South Cares, the charitable arm of the South Sydney Rabbitohs. Ms Keneally is the former Patron of Stillbirth Foundation Australia.

She holds a Bachelor of Arts (Honours) in Political Science and a Master of Arts in Religious Studies from the University of Dayton in Ohio. She has published many articles in academic and popular publications on religion, politics and feminism.

Kristina is married to Ben. They are the parents of Daniel, Caroline and Brendan.

The Interview

Karon: Senator Keneally, can you tell me how you and your husband Ben met.

Senator Keneally: We met at World Youth Day in Poland in 1991. I was there as a representative of the US Bishops Conference and Ben was there as a representative of the Australian Bishops Conference. This is pre-internet and pre-mobile phone time. I had graduated from university and was teaching primary school in rural New Mexico. Ben was finishing law school in Sydney. The house I lived in New Mexico didn't have a phone, so we were writing letters back and forth for the first year. We visited back and forth for a few years and I moved to Australia in September 1994. I applied for permanent residency through the old point system. It's very hard to do that these days, to apply as an offshore applicant for permanent residency. Back then it was straightforward. I filled out a few forms, documented my entire life, wrote a cheque for $450, and sent it off to the Embassy in Washington, DC. They gave me permanent residency based on that.

Karon: Can you share the circumstances of your baby Caroline's life and birth?

Senator Keneally: Caroline is our second child. Our first child Daniel was born in the United States where they didn't do ultrasounds as a matter of course in pregnancy. They only did them if they thought there was a problem. I went through my entire first pregnancy without an ultrasound. The pregnancy was quite easy, and Daniel was born two weeks late but a big, healthy newborn. We came back to Australia when Daniel was nine months old thinking we've got this nailed, we know how to have children. Not long after that, I fell pregnant with Caroline. The Australian system is quite different for pregnancy care. I had some bleeding problems early at six weeks and went to Hospital Emergency Department. They did an ultrasound and took issue with how far along I was. They thought the size of the baby indicated that I was not as far along as I thought, but I knew when I had fallen pregnant.

It seemed to be going along fine, then at the 18-week scan, it became obvious that Caroline had a congenital abnormality, which meant she wouldn't survive her birth and we had to make a decision about when I was going to give birth to her. I looked pregnant, I had a baby moving around inside of me, I felt pregnant, but there was no indication to the outside world or to how I felt that there was anything going wrong. Congenital abnormalities are still one of the most common causes of stillbirth. At 20 weeks I gave birth to Caroline. The decision was partly motivated by the fact I wanted to be sure that she didn't suffer and partly because I had a 13-month-old baby at home. I couldn't contemplate how I was going to look after him and continue with the pregnancy knowing my daughter wasn't going to survive. I think it was particularly difficult because I had gone through labour with Daniel, but I hadn't given birth to him naturally. I had a C-section. I was quite distressed at the idea that this had to be my first introduction to a natural birth.

What made it easier was the fact that we held her, named her, the priest blessed Caroline and the social worker came and we planned her funeral. We were allowed to spend as much time with her as we wanted. We created mementos, such as handprints and footprints, and photos. That meant a great deal to me because while she was only 20 weeks, she was our daughter.

I could have carried her to term, but I think it would have been a very difficult thing. Later I contemplated if I had carried her to term perhaps some of her organs could have been donated to another baby. I have at times wondered if I would have made another decision if I had thought about that. I've often thought maybe that's one good thing that could have come out of this. However, I don't think that I would have because it was so awful to contemplate. Living in the world, looking pregnant, and having people constantly ask me about the pregnancy, I couldn't contemplate how I would have coped knowing the baby was not going to survive. In the years since, I think good things still have come out of the experience of being Caroline's mother. I don't regret that. I also think you make the decisions you make at the time with the information you have. At that point, my biggest concern was her suffering. I knew from the doctor that there was less chance that she would feel any pain if I gave birth to her earlier in the pregnancy than going to term. Secondly, I had this little boy at home who needed a mother.

Karon: It must be incredibly difficult going through labour knowing that.

Senator Keneally**: I think the great horror of stillbirth for any woman who faces it, is knowing the baby is dead or is dying and will be dead when delivered. I think that's the hardest thing for the public to get their head around, and grapple with. It's not the tragic, horrible idea that a baby has died. You go through birth, knowing that the baby will be dead. That is a grief that is horrifying when you're going through it.** Then to talk about it to other people, they don't want to enter into it. I think the compounding tragedy with stillbirth is that people don't know how to talk about it with their family and friends. They don't know how to talk about it to the wider community, because they understandably can't comprehend what that must be like.

Birth is supposed to be new life and a joyful time. Maternity wards are meant to be happy places. Yet for the parents of a stillborn child, it is a terrible, horrible experience that is beyond comprehension for anyone who's ever been pregnant or welcomed a new baby into the world.

Karon: Normally in labour, we're able to think "This pain is terrible, but I'll see my baby at the end." But it's so different with stillbirth, isn't it?

Senator Keneally: It is. I had this weird disconnect, maybe it was the pain-relieving drugs and maybe it was my mind not comprehending what was happening. There's still that sense of anticipation "I'm giving birth, I'm going to see my child." When you're pregnant that's the one thing you can't wait for, to hold your child. At the same time there is a weird disbelief that my child will not be alive. There is a disconnect between your brain and your body. My body was giving birth and doing all the things that hormonally happen in birth. Your breasts produce milk even when the baby does not need it. **It is this bizarre, experience of hormonally being prepared and excited and anticipatory about your child arriving and this utter disjointed experience of being in complete and overwhelming grief that your child is dead.**

Karon: I've heard other mothers experiencing stillbirth hoped the doctors had got it wrong. That the baby was going to be born alive and everything would be okay.

Senator Keneally: Mothers have related to me, the doctor had said things that are almost confusing, like "We can't find the baby's heartbeat." Maybe the doctors think it's a gentler way of saying your baby has died. But it can leave the parents thinking, "Well, maybe they couldn't find it." One of the things I don't think we have done very well in Australia is train sonographers, clinicians, doctors, midwives, nurses, to have those conversations. I think we're getting better.

I was very fortunate I was at the Women's Hospital in Randwick. The doctor, who looked after me, was lovely. When Caroline was born, she said, "Oh, you little angel, you weren't meant for this world." It was a nice acknowledgment to a woman who had given birth that the doctors hadn't been wrong, and it was an acknowledgement that she was my baby.

Karon: She was a real little person, your baby.

Senator Keneally: Yes, absolutely [gently wiping tears away]. **We've changed quite a bit now. Mothers and fathers are encouraged to see their babies and to hold them.** I recall there was a politician in the US and he and his wife had a stillborn baby. They took the baby home for a few days. I know that there were people who thought that was weird, but I completely understood it. Death is one of those things that we have really sanitised and clinicalised. It wasn't all that long ago that people died at home and kept the body in their home. It was a natural part of life. Refrigerated cots have been developed that allow people to do that or to keep their baby in their hospital room for long periods.

A few months after Caroline was born one of my mother-in-law's friends related that her first child had been stillborn, and the baby was taken away immediately. She then was told to forget about it and to go home and have another one and heal. I can't even contemplate that. But that was the view then.

Karon: Some of those women were put away into psychiatric hospitals because they were grieving, which is sad. Those people never forgot their babies.

Senator Keneally: No, I did an interview a few years ago for *Australian Story* on stillbirth. What I couldn't believe was the number of letters I received afterwards from people who watched the show thinking it was going to be about me as a politician. It was a story about stillbirth. I'll never forget, what was relayed to me about how one couple sat watching the entire episode in silence: then for the first time in 40 years, spoke about their child. They decided they would go and try and find where he was buried. Another man wrote to say that his best friend saw it, called him up and said, "I know you know that politician and I need to tell you that my wife and I had a stillborn baby 30 years ago." This man was in his seventies. It's not good for the parents to not be able to talk about it. We're allowed to talk if your child is 18 and killed in a motorcycle accident. People come to the funeral; they talk to you about it; they mention your child by name. It's seen as a tragedy. But if it's a stillbirth, the parents are not given permission to talk about it. I don't think other people know how to talk about it with them.

In the Senate Inquiry into Stillbirth we were still hearing horror stories of things that professionals were saying to parents because they themselves didn't have the words and didn't have the experience of this tragedy. Then you get into situations like, whether or not parents will have an autopsy. Sometimes doctors are saying, "Oh, you probably won't learn anything, it's not worth going through the pain." I get why a doctor might say that to a family at this terrible point of grief. But on the other hand, there is so much a family might learn from having an autopsy. We had an autopsy with Caroline. I think for us, it was a straightforward decision. My husband's father is a doctor, his mother is a nurse. I'm very pragmatic. I wanted to know what had caused this, what the risks were because I wanted to have more children. When I got that autopsy report, it was almost a validation that she had been alive, that she was a person. It described her in very clinical terms, it was nonetheless the description of my child. For me it made Caroline seem more human and more real, that she had been alive.

My determination to have the Senate Inquiry has been validated by the overwhelming number of people who made submissions, and all the parents who were so determined that we do start talking about it. I think part of the reason we haven't done anything about stillbirth in this country is we don't talk about it. We pretend it's a private tragedy; we don't view it as a public health problem. Silence has been the biggest enemy in taking steps to reduce the incidence of stillbirth. Since we had the Stillbirth Inquiry, I've had people from all kinds of different contexts, contacting me to ask for examples; "My sister-in-law had a stillbirth, how do we react to her? What should we do, how can we be supportive?" I think there's recognition, but I still don't think people know quite what to do when it happens.

Karon: What advice do you give those people?

Senator Keneally: Well, the first thing I say is **learn the name of the baby and use it when you write them a card or a note. If it's a work colleague, I would suggest that maybe one person in the office contact them and say, "What are the practical things we can all do to help you?"** Try to find out if there's something they need. Make sure your workplace has paid parental leave which applies to stillbirth because a lot of workplaces still don't. It's not for lack of caring; I think it's for lack of not understanding that it's needed.

Karon: I was employed by New South Wales Health when my baby died, and my manager had to ring me and say, "Karon, we have to cancel your maternity leave, you can't have maternity leave when your baby dies." I had a week sick leave, but I needed three months off, so we had the added stress of financially struggling.

Senator Keneally: I would say people misunderstand that it's parental leave; it's not baby care leave. **There are things you need to do for a stillborn baby. Grief is one of those things, burying them is another, or having a cremation, memorialising them. You've given birth and you need to recover from all the physical effects of giving birth.** Parental leave is very important, you are a parent. It was one of the recommendations in the Stillbirth Inquiry. The Federal Government's Paid Parental Leave Scheme covers stillbirth and there are stillbirth payments. But there are still private sector companies that have failed to include it. It's not meanness, it's a lack of understanding that it needs to be done. **I also say to people, "Don't forget to talk about the baby in six months' time or in a year or into the future." The parents are not going to forget; it's their child. Don't be afraid to talk about the baby and use its name.**

Karon: You mentioned you had a funeral for Caroline. Can you tell us how you organised that?

Senator Keneally: We were very fortunate the funeral home didn't charge us, they said they did a service for stillborn babies for free, which is impressive in hindsight. I didn't think about it at the time. I was taken aback by everything that was going on because I'd never contemplated any of this. We had to pay for the cemetery plot which was $2000. Twenty years ago, that was a lot of money. I remember my husband and I were thinking "We're never going to spend any money on this child again." At the same time, you're thinking that's a big outlay of money on something you never expected.

Karon: And some families don't have that kind of money.

Senator Keneally: No, they don't. I don't think the stillbirth payment would cover the cost of a funeral in its entirety. One of the tragic revelations was that in rural and regional areas, there were some families that simply weren't having a funeral, or babies got left in morgues because they couldn't afford the cost of a funeral. That's horrifying to contemplate. There are babies in the Northern Territory that have been in the morgue six years.

Karon: Goodness. What is the thinking behind that?

Senator Keneally: They don't have any policy to deal with it. This is another area where we haven't really grappled with all these issues. There was a time when stillborn babies were treated like medical waste. I feel like there's such a hit and miss approach to this. Ben and I went to the nearest funeral home and they said, "Oh, no, we don't charge for stillborn baby's funerals." Whereas obviously there's a whole range of other responses; if there is no competition where they live, they get charged exorbitant amounts they can't afford. If the State doesn't have policy to deal with, it becomes this intractable problem.

Karon: Can you tell us a little bit about your grief experience, what was that like for you?

Senator Keneally: The grieving went on for quite some time. There were days I did not feel like getting out of bed. The only reason I did was because I had a child who needed a mother to get up and feed him and look after him. **There was a lack of joy, I felt like I was going through**

the motions. Before Caroline's birth I was working on my doctorate and I stopped because I had no interest at all in going back and sitting in a library, on my own, thinking great thoughts.

Previously I wanted to have four children close together but I didn't want to risk having another stillborn baby. We decided, all right, we will try to have one more. I fell pregnant within a year and had my third child, my second son, Brandon. **Being pregnant with him helped with the grief, but it was hard because I always felt on edge about whether this pregnancy would be okay. Even once we got past the point we had with Caroline; it was still nerve-racking.** Even after he was born, while I was quite happy about it, I was very sad a lot of the time.

Weirdly, September 11, 2001, knocked me out of it. I realised you've got these two kids, they're happy, they're healthy, you need to get on with life. There are things happening in the world. These kids need a mother to really be engaged with them. You need to be engaged with the world and there are things that you care about. I would say for a good two years, I was there without really being there.

Karon: People don't realise, with parental bereavement, it can take two to five years to return to a normal level of functioning. Not to recover, but to return to a normal level of functioning.

Senator Keneally: I think that's right. I may well have done so without a global tragedy to knock me to some movement. I distinctly remember sitting there in my house, watching the news coverage… the kids outside in the sandbox, I wasn't letting them near the television. Looking at them thinking there's a lot of sadness in the world and you can either stay in your grief or you can get up and look after these kids and make the world a better place. **I had been feeling a lack of purpose ever since I lost Caroline.** I had the purpose of being Daniel and Brandon's mother, but I didn't know if I had any other greater purpose. I don't want to make that sound like being a mother isn't a great purpose. I didn't know if my life was going to have anything else in it.

Karon: You hadn't even entered politics at that time, had you?

Senator Keneally: No, I'd been working on my doctorate. I had this whole plan for my life. I always wanted to be a professor. I gave it all up. I think it was a sense of wanting to feel useful to the world, but not knowing what that would be because everything about my life had changed. **The thing that had changed most dramatically was that I wanted to do things that made a difference to people's lives in a real, direct, impactful way,** in the way the social worker had helped me. I had a view that life is short and unpredictable. Your baby might die, you might be in an airplane that crashes into a building. I wanted to make a difference in ways that mattered. I wanted to get going soon and I didn't know what that was. I can't say that I said, "Oh, I'll run for politics," it wasn't that simple. But it was at that point that I realised I had been on autopilot, and lacking direction. Because everything had changed at that time when I lost her.

Karon: I don't think you ever see the world the same way again. And beliefs are challenged. I believe that you have a strong faith. Was that impacted by Caroline's life.

Senator Keneally: Oh, absolutely. **I couldn't understand why a loving God would take my baby away. While I found great comfort in the sense that her soul continued to exist, I thought it was wrong, that my baby wasn't with me.** Yes, there was anger. I reached that point, which is somewhat ironic, because my degree was in feminist theology. I'd written all these papers about the idea of God is mother. Then the Christian God is mother, and God is neither male nor female. Then one day I realised, if God is a mother, God is a mother whose child has died.

Karon: On the cross.

Senator Keneally: Exactly. As a Christian, I believe Jesus is the Son of God. If I also believe as it says, in the Bible, God is neither male nor female. I have spent all this time in an academic sense, extolling the maternal virtues of God. God is a mother whose child has died. God didn't intervene to stop the sense of free will and choices and the fact that God does not sit up there controlling the universe, like pieces of chess on the board. What that said to me is God can understand my grief and there is mercy that I can call upon and compassion. **God doesn't let things happen or not let things happen. I never really did believe in an interventionist God anyway**, but it really gave me a sense of comfort to think God is a mother whose child had died.

Karon: I can see how that would have given you comfort. As a mother to Daniel and Brandon, how did you cope as they grew up, and they had to go out and do things that might make a mother worry. Did you worry about their life?

Senator Keneally: No, if anything, I came to appreciate I can't control what happens. I can't wrap them in cotton wool. I can't stop bad things from happening to my children. They might happen, the world is unpredictable. I'm fatalistic, it's not that I didn't take care with them. But I probably had a more relaxed approach to them and the risks that we let them take. Kids need to learn to solve problems and take risks. When they arrive home from school and realise, they have left their key behind and they are locked out they need to solve that problem. My oldest son is a police officer and people often say, "Do you worry about him?" I say, well, no, because he's well trained, he's well resourced, and I can't worry about him all the time. Society doesn't work if people don't do these jobs. I'm proud of him for doing it.

Karon: During my research I noted you said that your husband, Ben, was very good at supporting you during your grief. Can you tell us about that?

Senator Keneally: **It must be very hard for fathers. There's the loss of their child and then there's the pain that they're watching their partner go through.** Whilst I don't think fathers feel the loss of their child any less acutely, it's undeniable that the mother had a physical connection to a baby. She went through surviving the birth and recovering from the birth. I think for fathers it's such multiple layers of grief. I think Ben was so patient with me, there was never any "You should," or "You must," or "You are too." It was letting me be whatever I needed to be. Whether it was cutting my hair off or not getting dressed the whole day.

Karon: He never judged you.

Senator Keneally: No, there was no judgment. For the first few months I slept with a blanket that Caroline had been wrapped in. There was no judgment about that, it was what it had to be. [As she gently wiped her tears away.]

Karon: People don't realise that you can still feel the pain and will for the rest of your life?

Senator Keneally: No, **it's been 20 years, but I still go to her grave every month. Every year on her birthday, I still pull out my box of mementos. We have a photo of her in our room.** Fifteen years ago, if someone said, how many children do you have, I would have said two. I now say, three. I saw a family a couple of months back in the cemetery and they were there with their two small kids and were visiting their stillborn baby's grave. They stopped to chat with me. They were like, "Wow, 20 years later." I said to them, "It's not going to go away, it's going to change. It will always be there."

Karon: I guess you learn to live with it.

Senator Keneally: Yes, and most of the time, it doesn't reduce me to tears any longer. I was elected to the Parliament four years after I lost Caroline and I mentioned her during my inaugural speech. It was about all I could do without bursting into tears. I'm not really a crier, I don't really cry at a lot of things. But somebody's loss of a child will always reduce me to tears. When we did the Senate Inquiry and produced the report in the Senate, a bunch of us spoke to it who were on the committee and I cried in that speech and it didn't bother me that I did. I cried not about my own child but because I read out the names of the children of the parents who appeared before that Inquiry and gave evidence. That's what got me in the end, those children and the bravery of their parents. When I lost Caroline, I didn't know anyone else this had happened to. I kept thinking; 'How did I not know about this? I'm smart, I have a Master's Degree, I've given birth before. How did I let this happen? Why am I so stupid?'

Karon: We all naively enter pregnancy and probably don't want to know this can happen. Do you feel that this is Caroline's legacy?

Senator Keneally: Well, it's not only hers. The thing that really struck me going to the Inquiry is that there were people who appeared, who are grandparents or older parents who lost babies decades earlier, there were parents who lost babies a few weeks earlier. It's their baby's legacy too. That's why I read each of their names out.

Karon: I believe that currently in Australia there are 2200 stillbirths a year, which is six per day, and the rate hasn't changed in 20 years! I guess you are hoping for that change.

Senator Keneally: I am delighted you have raised it. That statistic is right. There's no reason we can't change it. The Netherlands have seen a reduction of 60% over a decade and in Scotland a 35% drop. Britain has set a target of a 50% reduction by 2025. Teaching people to monitor foetal movements and know when they are changing, getting mothers to sleep on their side rather than their back reduces the incidence by 10%, and smoking and obesity are also risk factors. Understanding when to intervene in a pregnancy. There is no reason why Australia can't also see reductions.

Karon: In your speech you described Caroline's impact on you; "… **but she changed me forever. She enlarged my understanding of love and loss, and she taught me to survive. She made me brave, almost fearless."** Can you tell me about that?

Senator Keneally: When I ran for Parliament the first time, there were people attacking me and being vitriolic and I realised I didn't really care. They were calling me names. I remember saying to Ben, "So what. I have survived the most horrible thing I can imagine; I've given birth to my baby knowing she would be dead. I held her, I named her, and I buried her. This is nothing compared to that." I arrived at a point where I felt a sense of purpose and I was engaged with the world. Nothing could hurt me anymore than I had already been hurt. **There is strength that came from that experience. We have not given enough credit to women's strength that is born of surviving something awful and coming through the other side.**

If I could change what happened I would. It's not that I'm grateful this happened: I'm not. But something good did come out of it in the end and it turned me into a different person, a stronger one than I otherwise would have been. I think there is something to be said for people who have experienced a great loss. Having gone through a significant grief helps you cope with the ups and downs of politics with a bit of resilience. I think it also helps you cope with the complexities of human problems that come across your desk as a politician. People tell me significant and awful things that are happening in their lives and they are looking for help. It helps me understand where people are at and to have compassion for them.

Karon: The traumatic grief that comes from losing a child gives you a totally different perspective on life and empathy for others.

It has been an absolute honour to hear you so openly and honestly discussing Caroline's short life and death and sharing all that has come out of it. I hope I am smiling in the future looking at a reduction in the stillbirth statistics. Thank you so much.

In Remembrance – Caroline Keneally 18 June 1999

Key Concepts

Suddenly finding out your baby in your womb is not going to survive sends parents into a spinning state of shock and confusion. There is no obvious sign to confirm what they have been told. The pregnancy continues. In Kristina and Ben's case they then had to make a terrible decision; whether to continue the pregnancy or end it. This involved labouring knowing that Caroline was dead. This is a unique situation for the loss of a child where parents have to go through the most painful experience of giving birth.

All this can add to the possibility of the mother having posttraumatic stress disorder. A mental health condition that's triggered by a terrifying event — either experiencing it or witnessing it. Symptoms may include flashbacks, nightmares and severe anxiety, as well as uncontrollable thoughts about the event. Whilst this didn't happen to Kristina it is helpful to be aware of the possibility.

Creating memories with the baby is essential for there is no other time for these babies, no other memories for the parents. There is also a very limited time to do it. After the funeral is too late to think of these things.

Unique to parent's grief journey is that parents see themselves as providers and protectors for their children. To fail to protect your child from death is the biggest failure a parent can experience and is an assault to their self-esteem. It takes working through the irrational thoughts and beliefs to regain their self-esteem as a parent so they can effectively parent their living children.

Things that helped Senator Kristina's recovery:

1. "We held her, named her, the priest came and blessed her and the social worker came and we planned her funeral. We were allowed to spend as much time with her as we wanted. We created mementos, such as handprints and footprints, and photos. That meant a great deal to me because while she was only twenty weeks, she was our daughter."

2. The doctor supporting the delivery being empathic and recognised Caroline as a little soul.

3. Getting an autopsy gave them helpful information for future pregnancies.

4. Having Ben's unconditional love and acceptance without judgement.

5. Kristina allowed herself the space to grieve.

6. Knowing it's normal to feel like you are going through the motions of life while grieving.

7. Recognising it can take two to five years for parents to return to a normal level of functioning reassures the bereaved parent.

8. Understanding the pain and grief is not going to go away, it's going to change and become manageable. It will always be there.

9. Ensuring there was a Stillbirth Inquiry to change the system and reduce the number of stillbirths in Australia gave meaning to Kristina's experience and Caroline's death.

10. Going to Caroline's grave every month. Every year on her birthday, pulling out the box of mementos. "We have a photo of her in our room."

11. Examining her spiritual beliefs until she found peace.

12. Finding new strengths, courage and resilience in herself.

13. Taking action to take control of her life, finding a purpose and being engaged with the world.

Chapter 6

Julius Czerny

"None of us get out of life alive, so be gallant,
be great, be gracious, and be grateful for the
opportunities you have."

Jake Bailey

JULIUS CZERNY Biography

Author of the book, *Dead One Day. Laughing the Next,* public speaker, creator of triple international award-winning board game 'Super Life Saver', surf lifesaver, surf boat rower and survivor.

I am passionate and committed to reducing the number of avoidable fatalities by authoring a book about my death, revival and total recovery. My presentations highlight my important messages about recovering and moving forward from a fatal cardiac arrest which relates to everyone. I have created the board game aimed at mid to late primary school aged children to create early awareness of water safety, quick and appropriate response in emergencies. Because early education is the foundation for the future.

Julius received the Stevie Award
in London for his board game.

The Interview

Karon: Julius, can you tell me about the day you died?

Julius: Monday 6th of December was a lovely bright day we will remember for the rest of our lives. My wife, Helen and I live in Runaway Bay on the Gold Coast in Queensland. Runaway Bay is north of the Gold Coast, Tallebudgera is south of the Gold Coast a 30-minute drive from home. As a surf lifesaver I was a member rowing with a master surf boat crew, at Tallebudgera surf club. That particular morning, one of the junior crews that were training, had one of their lads unavailable to come. The guy that organised it rang me and asked if I could come in and fill in for them in the morning. I had the time, so I drove down to Tallebudgera and trained with the junior crew. We did a fair bit of hard work. It was half an hour drive down, probably an hour and a half rowing in the boat, and then driving home.

If my cardiac arrest hadn't happened at the time it did, I would have been in dire straits because having junior kids and being on the water, I don't think they would have been able to cope and been able to do the necessary resuscitation that would have saved me. In hindsight, I thought, "Wow, how lucky it didn't happen then." Or it could have happened while I was driving back from training. More recently, Ironman Dean Mercer, a surf lifesaver, was training for his Ironman in the gym at the Surfer's Paradise surf club. He finished his training, drove off, had a cardiac arrest as he was driving, crashed his car, and he wasn't able to be revived.

Karon: Oh, my goodness. You realise that could have happened to you?

Julius: When I look back, that could have been me. I trained in the morning, drove back, everything was fine. No symptoms, no signs, no nothing. Worked at our bakery all day, and then by 5 pm, I had to be back down at Tallebudgera for the training with the master's crew. On that particular day, the guy that steers the sweep was caught up at work. We got the message from him that we won't be in the boat at 5 pm and we need to transfer our training to the gym. The four of us met up there, had an hour of training organised for us and were given the program we had to do on the rowing machines. We completed one eight-minute effort at a fairly good pace and worked very hard. There were four rowing machines, we were side by side, and we rowed together. Having completed that one, we got up, walked around, rehydrated, recovered. Then we had two more to do.

I can recall sitting down on the rowing machine, strapping my feet in, and then lights out. That was it. There was no sign, no symptom, no, "Oh, my chest hurts," or "I'm sore down one side," or "I'm finding it hard to breathe." It was just snap and I was gone. At the time, the other three guys looked at me having fallen off the machine and realised, it's was not just me trying to get out of a training session. They were three qualified professional surf lifesavers with over 100 years of lifesaving experience between them, and they sprang into action. They knew what to do, they assessed me to have no pulse and I was going blue not breathing. They immediately began cardiac compressions and breaths and they weren't going to stop. This is what I've heard since.

Paul said he wasn't going to let my wife Helen have an awful Christmas and he kept begging me, "Come on Julius" as he frantically did the compressions. Graham drew the short straw. He did mouth to mouth finding it was difficult to keep my head tilted to open the airway.

Peter ran to the first aid room to get the defibrillator. The room was locked due to no volunteer patrol on the beach at 5.30 pm. He desperately searched for the keys but they couldn't be found. He quickly remembered the council lifeguard would be finishing his shift with a defibrillator in the patrol vehicle. He flagged him down outside the club at a red light. There was still no sign of life in me when they arrived with the defibrillator. They attached the pads and activated it. No response. "Stand back" and activated it again with no response. Again, and finally my heart responded. Two ambulances arrived soon after and the paramedics took over. My friends were exhausted from their 15 minutes of effort but relieved I was alive again. I knew nothing of what my crew had just been through but they had saved my life. I was awake and breathing. They told me "Helen is going to meet you at the hospital." My response, as they were putting me in the ambulance, was "What's wrong with her?" I had no idea what had happened. I thought, "Why is she going to a hospital? Is she not well?" I was completely oblivious to the fact that I'd had a cardiac arrest, had died, and been resuscitated. That was just a blank spot. Not that I woke up and thought, "Where have I been? What have I done?" No, I just woke up and thought, "Here I am."

Karon: Had your GP diagnosed you with any heart disease?

Julius: No.

Karon: You had absolutely no idea?

Julius: No idea at all.

Karon: Helen can you tell me about your experience on the day that Julius died?

Helen: It was just a normal business day, and Julius normally trains and does whatever he wants to do. He was out and about doing what he normally does. The first I knew about it was when I got a call from Graham, one of the men who resuscitated Julius. He didn't tell me what happened. He just said, "You have to get in your car and go to hospital." I replied, "Which hospital?" He said, "I don't know, just get in your car and start driving because both hospitals are south of you." When I got in my car, I rang my mum and discussed with her what could have happened because he didn't give me any indication. He didn't say Julius had a heart attack. Julius has cut his arm, or broken his leg or whatever. I just thought, "I don't know what's happened."

Karon: That's a bit scary?

Helen: It was a bit scary.

When Graham rang me, he told me the ambulance was there. My mum was saying to me, "The best thing is that you know that he's in the best place. If the ambulance is there, that is the best thing that can happen." She was trying to reassure me. As I drove, I got a call back from Graham to say go to the Gold Coast Public Hospital. I still didn't know what happened. I rang Kate, Julius's daughter. She's nearby to there so she came in with her boyfriend. When we arrived, we were taken to a very nice room away from emergency. They said a counsellor will come in and talk to you. Up until then we were frightened not knowing what had happened. Then we were all told what happened and we knew that everything was all right because somebody had told us he's stable, he's in the ambulance. We actually got there before Julius did which is a bit weird. But she said, "I've spoken to the ambulance driver and she told us he is stable. This is what's happened to him."

Then she told me exactly what the procedure would be once he arrived. Soon after Julius arrived and when I saw him, he looked fine. Up on the wall they've got a screen, listing all the critical patients and he was number one. Then someone else came in and went in front of him. **When something like that happens, it's very surreal. I guess your body just goes into fight-mode, the adrenaline and everything. It's hard. You're taking things in, but you're not really... there's no emotion to it.** That's how I felt anyway, until afterwards. Yeah. It's probably more the next day and that night.

Karon: What do you mean by, "Until afterwards, and that night"? What happened then?

Helen: I left Julius at the hospital once he had to have the angiogram and stent put in, which was about 10 pm that night. Then I got a phone call from Graham and he started to tell me a little bit about what had happened and filled me in about the details. I guess I went to bed thinking, what if? what if? In my mind I'm thinking, "Oh my God, that could have happened first thing this morning." I know it didn't, but in my mind, I just kept re-running things that could have happened. I didn't sleep very well that night and then the next morning, Graham and Deirdre, his wife, came and picked me up because, Julius' car was down at Tallebudgera. I collected his car and then we all went to the hospital. There were quite a few of the guys turned up that day.

Then Julius got to hear the story of what happened and their interpretation of the stressful situation for them. Fifteen minutes of reviving somebody is such a long time. Stinky (Paul), said to me, "The whole time I was saying, 'Come on Julius, we can't let this happen you've got to be able to breathe; you've got to stay with us.'"

Julius [laughing]: Because he wanted to win the surf boat races that were coming up.

Helen: No. I guess, hearing their side of the story was pretty traumatic and even for Julius probably now, it's still traumatic. They told us every little detail of what happened. I could really see that Graham really struggled with it a lot. Deidre, his wife told me that he had counselling. Because to see somebody dead and revive them is pretty stressful. The next day you hear the whole story and that's where the emotional side comes in. It just becomes very draining and hard to hear.

Julius: I think Graham was distressed and really upset about it because he's the one that gave me mouth to mouth. Now that would be very distressing, I think.

Helen: Yes, I think so.

Karon: And did he have the plastic sheet to put over your mouth?

Helen: No, no, no.

Julius: We were good friends. We've won a few major titles together so we're better friends now.

Karon: As a Registered Nurse myself, I've been involved in numerous resuscitations on people I don't know. These were your mates resuscitating you!

Helen: I know. Like I said, Paul was very adamant. He was pleading, "Julius, you cannot… it's not your time. You got to stay here. You've got Helen." He said he talked to him the whole time because he was the one doing compressions.

Julius: Fifteen minutes of that. That's hard work there.

Helen: That's hard work. Paul said to me, "Helen, if this had happened at home, there is no way you could have saved Julius. It was so hard just to get through his chest and everything. He's a pretty big fellow." These guys luckily are big fellows too. Hearing that the next day I thought, "Oh my goodness." Just the what-ifs and the emotional side of things, it was quite emotional really.

Julius: I sort of look back on the scene as well thinking, "I can't imagine how Helen would have felt having to drive to the hospital not knowing what's going on. I can't imagine what was going through her head thinking what the scenario could have been. What the heck could I be doing there? What's the best-case scenario? What's the worst-case scenario? Just not knowing, I think that would be... that would have rocked me. The other thing that occurred to me was we were meant to be rowing out in the ocean that day, but because one guy couldn't arrive, it changed that. If the cardiac arrest had happened when we were two kilometres offshore, there's no way known they would have been able to do the resuscitation properly. It would have been ten minutes to get back to shore, and then get me from the shore into the surf club, and then call for assistance.

The other thing was we could have done that first eight-minute phase and finished. I could have got in my car, driven off and been like Dean Mercer and have the cardiac arrest in the car on my way home. I would have had a passenger with me. I could have killed both of us. The stars just aligned that things worked the way they did. People say you're lucky. I don't like using luck and death in the same sentence, but it was. One of those people said, "You're lucky you were in the surf club." I'll maintain it's not really luck; I've been involved with surf clubs for 50 years. It was a lifestyle choice. I was lucky I was only in hospital for three days. Again, that's because I've looked after myself all these years and that's why I wasn't sitting in hospital for three weeks as a lot of other people would be.

Helen: Yes, and back to work because I rostered you on, on Saturday.

Julius: I was admitted on Monday. Had the angiogram and stent put in on Monday night, and on Tuesday I was saying. Well, even when they wheeled me into the hospital, they told me, "Oh, you've had..." And I'm saying, "You are kidding. Rubbish, I'm fine. We're going home." And they said, "No, you're not going home." I didn't feel a thing. There were no residual effects from it at all."

Helen: Just your tongue.

Julius: My tongue was a bit funny. I think, when I fell off the rowing machine, I may have bitten my tongue. I don't think Graham bit my tongue [laughing]. Also, the next few days I was saying to the cardiologist, "I still feel a bit tight and a bit sore in the chest." He said, "That's because this guy was jumping up and down on you for 15 minutes." I said, "Well, that was understandable." But apart from that, nothing. The next day I was saying to the nurses and doctors, "Well, I can go home. I'm fine. There's nothing wrong with me." I said there were people waiting for beds and so on and obviously in more desperate need than I was to have a bed in the hospital. Besides, I didn't like the food much anyway.

The fact is on the Thursday of that week, we had a Christmas function to go to, and I wanted to go to the Christmas function. All the signs were good and I think they were sick of me whinging about not wanting to be there. On the Thursday they relented.

Karon: That's amazing.

Julius: Helen had me rostered for work on the Saturday.

Karon: We often hear about people having seen a white light or, having what's called a near-death experience when they die. Did that happen to you?

Julius: Well, people ask me, "Is there anything on the other side?" I can honestly say, "There may be, but they showed me nothing." I didn't even know I'd gone. I didn't feel, "Oh, here it comes or…" Just, bang, gone. The next thing I'm waking up on the gurney as they're putting me in the ambulance. Absolutely, nothing.

Karon: It sounds like you got on with your life from day three.

Julius: Yes, it was just a hurdle, and I overcame that hurdle, and moved on.

Karon: Did you have any fears, in the months after the heart attack that it might happen again?

Julius: No. My thought was if it happens again, hopefully, I'll be with surf lifesavers again and they might be able to do the same thing. But if not, well, I cheated death once, that's a pretty good score. If it happens again and I don't happen to cheat death, be that as it may. And not many people have two birthdays in the one year, which I now claim; I have one in July and one in December. I went to the gym as soon as I could. I was keen to get back into rowing, and we actually won a race three weeks later and I had been training for that.

Karon [surprised]: You were back in a race three weeks later?

Julius: We raced and we won. When we were on the dais receiving our award the other crew that came second, came racing up and lodging a protest, saying "He's been surgically enhanced." That was a quite humorous anecdote to the whole thing. But, for a little while, I used to walk around the rowing machine, saying to myself "Oh, those things, they can kill you." It's something that I've been on consistently since, I haven't let up.

I regularly had appointments with the cardiologist and I did the cardiac tests and the treadmill tests. That was fairly soon after. I got the results and everything was well above average and I said to the cardiologist, "Well, am I all right to row? I need the okay because it's a policy of lifesaving." In the end, he said, "Well, until you get the okay, you can't compete." This is after we'd actually won the race. I said to the cardiologist, "I need to get the okay." "Oh, no, no, no, not for three months." I go, "You are kidding me." And then I said, "All right." Then he gave me the test results. I quickly made an appointment with my GP, took in the test results, and I said, "Doc, have a look at these. Are they pretty good results?" He said, "Yes they are really good." I said, "You think I'd be right to row?" He said, "Well, no problem." I said, "Well, sign this." He did, so I pulled that one. But I don't tell the cardiologist that because I scammed him. But I was back into it and haven't stopped since. Do I fear? No. My philosophy is, if it is to be, it is to be. It wasn't my time. When my time does come, there's really not a lot I can do about it. I didn't even know I'd gone. I could have just been gone and I would have been none the worse off. But people around me, those people would have been affected. I'm very conscious of that. But I sometimes ring the three guys that revived me and I say, "You know, bugger you guys, I now have got to go through old age because of you. I could have avoided it." Tongue in cheek. But there's still plenty that I want to do and I'm going to be going for a while yet, if that's the way it's meant to be.

Karon: Well, that's a wonderful attitude. But as you say, it's easy for the person who dies; it's the people left behind that suffer. How has it affected you, Helen?

Julius: She would have been a lot richer if I had died due to our insurance.

Helen: I would have. We got a bit of a payout, but we get more if Julius dies. As Julius said, he got a stent so his heart works better now than it did before.

Julius: My artery was 98% blocked and that would have happened over a period of time. I figured, "I'm better off than I was." That's why the cardiologist wants me to take statins and aspirin, and I said, "Well, you can put those where the sun don't shine because I'm not going to be taking them."

Helen: No. And, you know, he takes fish oil every day, krill oil, so his blood's thinner. We watch what we eat and we do all sorts of things like that because we believe that food is medicine. My view is the same as Julius, if something's going to happen and it's your day, so be it. Life is like that. If it's your time to go, it's your time to go. I'm not religious. Julius was brought up Catholic, but, that's just life. You're not in control of every single part of your life. A lot of things you are, but some things you're not. If one of us dies, we'll move on. We've both spoken about that... and maybe because of the heart attack, we have spoken about those things now. I don't want him to wallow and be unhappy for the rest of his life and he doesn't want me to either. We've got a pretty optimistic lookout on life. You're here, you need to enjoy it. If you're not here...

Karon: Sounds like you've had that conversation where you've given each other permission to move on and get a new partner if the other dies?

Helen: Of course.

Julius: Well, we will both be upgrading [laughing].

Karon: **That makes a huge difference to somebody in bereavement, knowing what their partner wanted for them.**

Helen: Yes. And it's funny you say that because we've spoken about those things. Just recently, my dad died earlier this year and my mum and dad hadn't spoken about some of those things. I would say to mum; dad would want you to be happy... He wouldn't want you to just wallow in his death. They hadn't had that conversation. Not everybody has that conversation. I thought they did as they were getting older, but obviously people don't. But we certainly have. We've talked about all sorts of things like that, as far as getting older.

Karon: Well, that's great that you've done that. But there's another amazing thing that you've done, Julius. You've created an amazing legacy from your experience. Can you tell us about that?

Julius: I thought I could tell my story and share my message in a book. I've been a certified surf lifesaver for 50 years now. My book, *Dead One Day, Laughing the Next*" has three messages. One: Know CPR [cardiopulmonary resuscitation]; have people around you know CPR; have some sort of a backup. Two: Have Trauma Insurance. Mine paid handsomely. I mean, the premiums are really high, but I got a 600% return on my investment. The third message is to keep yourself in good health so that your body can recover, which is also vital.

Helen: You have done lots of public speaking to get your message out.

Julius: Most of them were voluntary and I've done that to get things going, get the ball moving. I've also created a board game for kids, early education being fundamental. Then we spent a lot of time going around Australia to education events to promote the board game. It's directly related to the DRSABCD [a first aid action plan] chart. It's creating awareness so that when the kids grow up with it, they're more likely to respond appropriately rather than the small percentage of people that now respond appropriately. The reason that there are a lot of fatalities is because of inappropriate or lack of bystander response. If there was more bystander response, we would decrease the number of fatalities, no question.

Karon: That's very true, but I'm sure you've had an impact on the outcomes since 2010. Have the statistics changed?

Julius: **Well, when I had my cardiac arrest the statistics in Australia were 4% survival of out-of-hospital cardiac arrests. Now, it's up to 10% and that's attributed to the fact that there is a little bit more**

education and certainly because of more defibrillators. In Seattle, when you renew your driver's license, you have to renew your CPR.

Karon: Wouldn't that be great if it happened in Australia?

Julius: Yes. Worldwide, the average is 10% survival rate. In Seattle, and a couple of other States like New York and in Denmark, the survival rate is up to 60%.

Karon: Wow. That's a huge difference,

Julius: And that's my push at the moment. I've donated games to many surf clubs and schools. The same with a lot of the hotels and high-rise apartment buildings on the Gold Coast for kids to play on holidays.

Karon: That's fantastic. It's lovely that you've made such a difference. Helen, can I ask you one last question? Do you have anything that you want to add as the partner? Any advice you would give to people in terms of coping afterwards?

Helen: Coping afterwards. To me it's probably that family thing of having a relationship with your family. I'm pretty close to my mum and dad. I think that is important.

Karon: Because you get support from them in difficult times?

Helen: Yes. I'm also a believer that food is medicine. We have looked at the reasons why this happened to Julius. I'm into researching reasons why and then adjusting your food accordingly.

Karon: Thank you both so much for your time and wisdom and sharing your traumatic experience.

Key Concepts

Experiencing the sudden and unexpected death of yourself through heart attack, as Julius did, is a big wake up call to most people that life is short and can be taken away at any time. It impacts the whole family as well as those around them. In this case the friends who resuscitated him were also affected for a long time. It can cause anxiety and depression in some as they fear dying suddenly again. It also causes people to wonder what comes after death, if there is an afterlife.

It can be used as an opportunity to reflect on who and what is important in life and to evaluate if you are living the life you want to live or if there needs to be some adjustments.

Things that helped Julius's recovery:

1. Having a supportive wife in Helen.

2. Helen found the support of her family essential.

3. Having the friends debrief and tell him and Helen the details of what happened.

4. Having lived an active life Julius was in a healthier state which helped him recover more quickly.

5. He and Helen researched the reasons why this happened to Julius and then adjusted their diet, as they believe 'food is medicine'.

6. Having trauma insurance.

7. Creating a legacy by writing a book and talking about the importance of everybody learning CPR to groups. He wanted his experience to be of value to others.

8. Creating the triple international award-winning board game 'Super Life Saver' to help children understand CPR.

Chapter 7

Susan Templeman MP

FEDERAL MEMBER FOR MACQUARIE

"When we meet real tragedy in life, we can react in two ways – either by losing hope and falling into self-destructive habits or by using the challenge to find our inner strength."

14th Dalai Lama

SUSAN TEMPLEMAN MP Biography

Federal Member for Macquarie

Susan Templeman is the Federal Member for Macquarie, the largest electorate in the Sydney region; encompassing the Blue Mountains and the Hawkesbury. She was first elected in 2016 and again in 2019.

Susan, and her husband Ron, have lived in the Blue Mountains for over 25 years.

A former radio journalist and foreign correspondent in New York and London, Susan ran a media and presentation training company with clients spread across the country for more than 20 years, before becoming the Federal Member.

Susan has long been an advocate for her community, on issues such as education funding, mental health and support for local businesses.

She understands the importance of the beautiful natural local environment of the Hawkesbury and Blue Mountains and is determined to protect the World Heritage National Park that surrounds this unique area.

Her family, like hundreds of others, lost their home in the 2013 Winmalee bushfire. Susan and her husband rebuilt on the same site.

Since taking up her role as Federal Member in 2016, Susan has unreservedly championed the causes that matter to the people of Macquarie in the Federal Parliament.

Susan sitting amongst the rubble of her home after the bushfires.

Photo by Peter Rae, Sydney Morning Herald

The Interview

Karon: Thank you so much for your time Susan. Where were you when you heard about the fires in the Blue Mountains in October 2013?

Susan: My husband Ron and I had been working in the city and we hit the road having heard that there were fires. Our 19-year-old son, Harry, was at home, and we spent probably an hour and a half being with him remotely as he was identifying there was a fire. Identifying the severity of it. Helping him work out what he needed to take. Then saying "Get out of the house now. Go!" Within about 15 minutes of him leaving the house, he sent us a text message that said, "It's gone." And I said to Ron, "Listen to what he said. 'It's gone.' He must be talking about the house. But how would he know? He's at the Winmalee shops."

I texted back and said, "What do you mean, 'It's gone'?" We couldn't get voice communication very easily, but we could get text through. When we did speak to him maybe 15 minutes later, I said, "What do you mean 'It's gone'?" He said a neighbour saw the house on fire when they left and told him at the shops where they'd all been rendezvousing. We were in the middle of the M4 motorway. It was a completely bizarre situation. I thought, "Okay, we're driving home to a house that's no longer there, our son is at the shops, he's alive. But something big is happening in the mountains." It was a weird experience and not very real. We didn't instantly feel massive disappointment. We didn't know what to feel. We were in shock, I think, at that point.

But I think what shaped my thinking about it was something that happened during that journey. We were listening to the ABC on the radio, we had two phones with text messages coming and going. I had my iPad and was looking at Facebook. A post popped up in my feed and it was an old friend. Someone who was a workmate back in the '80s and he said, "Thank you all so much for your comments about Nathan. It's a terrible loss but we're so proud that we had him." I went, what's this about? It didn't make any sense and it turned out that his son, who was a similar age to our kids, had been killed in a motorbike accident a couple of days before and I hadn't been aware of it. I said to Ron, "Oh, my god. Look at this." That instantly put into context the loss that we were going through. It really shaped how I thought about the fires because at that point, no one was dead. It was a house that was gone but not the loss of a person. Our daughter Phoebe was in Sydney. She wasn't living at home at that stage. She wasn't in any danger whatsoever.

Karon: That put it all in perspective for you? It's different when you've still got all your family, isn't it?

Susan: I cry even when I think about it now. It was formative in the way I thought and dealt with what happened in subsequent days.

Karon: What happened when you arrived in Springwood?

Susan: We couldn't get to Springwood. We worked out that we had to go via Yarramundi and come up Hawkesbury Road. Our main aim was to get to Harry at the Winmalee shops. Ron dropped me there. I don't even know whether he stopped to see Harry. He then kept driving towards our house at Winmalee. There were roadblocks and he pulled over and started walking. The police wouldn't let him into the street. He and another neighbour decided they were going to go in anyway. They were appropriately attired and in they went. Ron got in there a few hours before me and he started activating the Community Fire Unit to try and save some houses that were burning. The fire had moved through but there were the embers that had got into roofs, there were still lots of small fires to be put out.

A few hours later, as the night was starting to settle, we got word people were able to go back to their homes. Harry and I drove back up Hawkesbury Road. Our cat, Sass, was still in the car. We got as close as we could, pulled over and walked into our street. Harry and I kept going, "Oh, my God. It doesn't look like our street anymore." And the thought going through my mind was that the only thing I could compare it to was that it reminded me of a scene I had seen of Sarajevo after being bombed in that conflict. It was surreal. It was twilight. Walking through the dust and smoke, the haze and the smell of it. Walking past burnt-out cars, then walking down to our place, and seeing my car sitting there, because we'd been in Ron's car that day working in the city together. My car, my

Peugeot 307, was parked at the top of the house, and it was this melted tangled mess with the aluminium melted to the ground. extraordinary. It was very confronting. It took my breath away. It was hard for my brain to process what had happened and how it had happened. There was nothing left. Our house was timber; all that was left was a tangled mass of metal. All the timber had burned and the ground was still very hot. There were still things smouldering. A mess of broken china and tangled unrecognisable stuff. Even the next morning when Channel 9 came and all the TVs were there, I had to warn Karl Stefanovic, "Be careful because it's actually still quite hot there."

October 17 dawned hot and dry with wind gusts of up to 100kmh. At 2 pm fire broke out near Linksview Road at Springwood and crossed Hawkesbury Road within 30 minutes and burnt through Springwood, Winmalee and Yellow Rock. The speed and intensity of the fires was beyond human control. Three hours later 195 homes had been destroyed and 146 buildings damaged. As night fell, it became clear that nearly entire streets had been wiped out by the Linksview Road fire at Winmalee and Yellow Rock. Surprisingly no one was dead. October 20 the NSW Premier declared a State of Emergency as weather conditions were forecast to worsen in the coming days.

Karon: Where did you stay that night, you, Ron and Harry?

Susan: Well, funny story that. Harry was 19 and on a gap year. He was working but he planned to go to Byron Bay for the weekend. At about 7 pm, Harry and I went around to my mum's place. She lives in Springwood, but Mum and Dad were away for the weekend in the Hunter Valley. I hadn't texted Mum but she texted me. When I finally spoke with her, she said, "Go to my place." And I said to her, "Well, I'm already here. I haven't had a chance to tell you that." And she said, "Oh, I heard on the radio that the fire hurt you. People have been telling me that your house burned down." We were lucky. Mum and Dad live only a couple of kilometres away. Ron stayed in the street till close to midnight I think, helping do clean up and stuff. But Harry and I went around there. When we got there, I said to Harry, "Look, there's nothing here for you. You had plans (to go away for the weekend). Do you still want to go?" He replied, "Look, I might as well." Everyone was in shock. And I'm not sure if that was the best decision but it was his decision to go. Ron joined me a bit later at Mum and Dad's and that's where we spent the night. We instantly had somewhere to go. We didn't have that terrible uncertainty that a lot of people had which was, "Oh my God. Where are we going to sleep tonight?"

Karon: You talked about it being surreal. Did you have that feeling that a lot of people experience, that you were in a dream and you hoped you would wake up from it soon?

Susan: I don't know. I do remember in the morning waking up and going, Oh, God. That's what happened. **I remember being in shock. For me it was like walking through fog. You don't really realise you're in fog until it starts to lift and then you go, Oh, I've been in a fog, haven't I?** I don't know there's a lot of self-awareness around that. But what I did notice was my world shrunk and I could only focus on a few things, and the one thing that I could focus on was work, thinking, "Well, I have to be back at work on Monday." And because I'd been at work, I had my work gear with me. A lot of it got destroyed but I had basics with me. My focus was, "Gosh, I'm going to have to work really hard now so that we've got money to recover from this thing that's happened to us." I didn't really think about a lot else. It took me until Christmas time, to feel like the fog was lifting a bit. To feel a bit more human. I had to keep functioning. I was back at work with clients on the Monday. I was wearing a work dress when that fire happened. Then I pulled it out to put it on and I went, "Oh, my goodness, it still smells like smoke." I hadn't even thought about throwing it in the washing machine. And I said to my clients, "Look, I still smell a bit smoky." But the client specialised in working with people with mental health conditions. I said to them laughing, "This is probably the perfect place for me to be. If I fall apart as the day goes on, you'll know what to do."

Karon: Did you have any short-term grief when you recognised the possessions you had lost?

Susan: **Oh yes, absolutely. Waves of it. I couldn't predict when it was going to happen. I might be walking down the street in Springwood and all of a sudden, I've seen someone, and they'd say something and boom, it's being engulfed in this blaze of grief. I think a lot**

of us got used to saying to people, "Oh, look, I cry a bit now; I'm okay but I cry." I think that happened for months and months and months, probably a year. There were a few times I remember going to a place where my feelings were uncontrollable. Not a lot and only on my own.

Karon: When you said you'd talked to your mum, I thought, "Oh, I would have been in tears once I talked to my mum."

Susan: I think I was okay. I knew she'd be upset, and my main aim was to say to her, "No, we are all okay. We are all fine. It's all gone but we're okay." That was the focus for that first few days. We are all okay. The possessions didn't seem that significant at that point. It was probably later where I went, "Oh, damn. I've lost my violin and irreplaceable things like jewellery from my father's mother. Harry managed to get a bunch of photo albums out but we lost a box of photos that had never made it into albums. Whole chunks of the kids' history are gone.

Karon: Did you ask yourself, "Why us? Why our home when they were homes left standing beside completely burnt down homes?"

Susan: I don't remember asking that question. I remember going, "Wow, how did that home survive?" But not, "Why didn't ours?" I would think there was some logic in there. Our house was a Western red cedar timber pole home and if any house was going to go in a bushfire it was going to be ours. I think that was more likely a question for the more recent people who built very solid brick houses. I think we always felt when you live in the Mountains, that this is the risk you're taking. I'm unlikely to get hit by a tsunami but chances of a bushfire are reasonably high, and there's a small chance that it might take your home and a remote chance that it'll really impair your lives. I think there was some logic kicked in there that stopped us from going down that path.

Karon: What was the rebuilding process like for you and your family?

Susan: Slow. It was slow You're a different person as you go through whatever the journey is. The first thing was to decide whether we wanted to rebuild. It was our instinct to do it, and then we went, "But hang on. We're in shock, is this really the right thing to do?" We took a bit of time to think about that. It took us about a year before we absolutely took a step and then there was no turning back. We'd had plans drawn but we went, "Oh well, we don't have to proceed and we've got the DA in, but we don't have to proceed." I think we didn't trust that we were making a decision that wasn't tinged with our reactions to the fire. We wanted to make sure that it was the right thing to do. We really couldn't find anywhere else that appealed to us to live at all. We kept coming back to the community going, "We really want to be in the Mountains." My logic was, "Well, if we buy somewhere else in the Mountains, what's the bet that's where the next bushfire will hit, knowing our luck." We worked on the theory that lightning rarely strikes twice. But we were slow. We didn't have any kids at home. We rented something very affordable and we were able to help Harry out in Sydney to get himself established there for attending University. We knew people with kids at school probably were in a hurry. They probably really needed to get their kids back into their normal routine and live close to schools. We thought, "Well, there'll be a real rush for tradespeople, so we'll take it easy and let it happen slowly."

Karon: You were the Labor candidate for Macquarie and had lost in the Federal election only the month before. That's two major losses so close together.

Susan: I lost in the September 7, 2013 election. Five weeks later, the house burned down as I was sort of getting over the election. The election takes a while to recover from. We didn't have another election till 2016. That was a little while away and we weren't back in the house then. We didn't get into the house until 2018. It took us nearly five years to get back in.

Karon: I guess there was a recovery period anyway, wasn't there?

Susan: Yes. By the time we moved back in, we were so ready. We were champing at the bit. Whereas conversations I've had with some people suggests that they were a bit disinterested in what their new home looked like when they rushed into it. It wasn't until sometime after they moved in, they realised, "I don't like these. And I don't know why I chose these taps, or this fan, or whatever." Because they were doing it so soon after they lost everything, and they had to build to a strict new building code.

Everything we did, we think, has led us to make quite good decisions. Financially, the slow pace of it meant that we were able to sell an investment property that allowed us to build the sort of house that our insurance wouldn't have allowed us to build. We've ended up investing a lot more back into the block than we would have been able to do had we relied on the terrible amount of insurance that we had.

I saw people having terrible loss with the fire. Then they had their hopes of rebuilding shattered by not having enough insurance money and terrible financial pressure to try and work out how to rebuild something and salvage something out of it. I saw people that were sort of hit while they were down, as it were. Whereas while we were in a similar situation of not having enough insurance to rebuild, we had an alternate avenue. That was all good luck. It means Ron can never really retire because that was his retirement. But we made a choice about living now rather than worrying about what's going to happen in the future.

Karon: Communities are often more resilient than we expect at times of tragedy. I'm wondering what was your impression of how the Blue Mountains community dealt with this fire?

Susan: I think it was one of the biggest natural disasters in New South Wales. The community was so giving. People kind of sprang into action from what I could see. One of the things I noticed was, I'd come home to my mum's place and I'd find a suitcase of clothes there that someone had dropped off. Or there'd be a box of groceries or all sorts of things that people were incredibly generous in sharing. That sort of generosity blows your mind. I think that helped. It did teach me one thing. At the initial point of crisis, people absolutely need the basics. You don't care what you have. Any toothbrush will do and any toothpaste and any shampoo. But then a little while further in you go, "Actually, I'd really like my shampoo now." Your brain's sort of going, "Hang on. This isn't the toothpaste I actually choose when I get a choice." There comes a point where you're ready to start making your own decisions. These five phases of recovery where initially you don't care. Anything, thank you. That's a T-shirt. "Yeah, that'll do." But as you go on, you start to go, "Well, no. Now I have the capacity to choose." It's an interesting process to go through.

After three or four weeks, when we were moving into our rental property, one of the organisations gave us Kmart vouchers. We had an absolute ball going through Kmart with a shopping trolley, choosing the garbage bin that we wanted and the tea towels that we wanted in our new little rental place. And there were moments of revelation that come when you realise, "Yeah, I'm ready to make a decision."

Karon: That means for people wanting to do something, the best thing they can do, is provide money?

Susan: **It has led me to feel, as generous as it is when people want to give some clothes and toys and things (depending on where people are in the event that's overtaken them); giving cash allows people to make decisions for themselves.** Also, you feel constantly grateful and required to express gratefulness. You're totally grateful for what people have done but you get weary of constantly thanking people. It's a funny feeling. I mean, people made meals and extraordinary stuff. The other thing is different people need different things at different times. And the natural disaster might have occurred commonly to a whole group of people, but how we move away from it is completely individual, even within families. Someone might love having meals prepared for them for weeks and weeks and weeks. And someone else might go, "What? I want to get in the kitchen and cook myself and my family a meal." That wasn't me but Ron wanted to. I have this theory that the extraordinary generosity was because everybody who didn't lose their house in the Mountains thought, "Oh, my God. That could have been me."

Karon: I believe that is true. I certainly did as I live in the Blue Mountains.

Susan: We all know it could have been any of us, had the wind done something slightly different. I think everyone empathised and related so strongly to people but that's why we had a particularly generous community. Then you had a bunch of people who aren't used to receiving charity, struggling a bit with how to receive it and how to accept it. That was a duality happening there. There was a story on the front page of the *Sydney Morning Herald* a few weeks into it all, where the Salvation Army and other charities were commenting on the fact that it was really hard to get people to accept money or significant support because we said, "Oh, no, no. There are people much worse off than me. You should go to them." But there did come a point I think where most people went, "No. This has been bad and I could do with some help." You get to that point of accepting.

Karon: Looking back now from where you are, would you have any advice for people who lose their homes in the future? Did you develop helpful strategies that you'd like to share with people?

Susan: **The number one thing is, make sure that if a disaster hits, you're well enough insured so that you don't find yourself being hit by a double whammy. Ensure you can rebuild or relocate, and you have the wherewithal to move on from the event.** Whether that means physically moving on or use it as an opportunity to rebuild the house you always wanted. But I think the practical thing that you can do is not make it worse by being underinsured. That's not necessarily easy. It's hard to do but it's worth the effort. What worries me now is that those who went through it get it, and everyone else has a vague understanding of it but I'm not sure that it means everyone's reviewed their insurance and has the level of insurance that they need.

The other thing, especially if you're in a bushfire area, is think about the things you can live without and the things you can't live without. If you really think there are things that you don't want to lose, well, think about how you save those or copies of them. The big thing people saved is the photos. Losing their family photos and even photos that they were custodians of, for the wider family, grandparent's photos and family history photos, all that boring stuff of getting them up in the cloud. I can see people really valued being able to replace photos and things like that. It's not very exciting but it's that preparation of the physical stuff.

Then there's the mental preparation of thinking, what's important to me, and working your brain through that exercise. **Asking yourself, "At the end of the day, does any of this stuff really matter?" And for us the answer was, no. It's lovely to have but, so long as we've all got our lives, we can go on and you find you get new stuff quickly.** It'd be fascinating to talk to people now. I'm much more careful about what I buy, but we have still accumulated, in the six years since it happened, a huge amount of stuff. I think some mental preparation if you live in an area that is prone to disaster is really useful.

Karon: Perhaps talk about, what if it happens to us and then develop your strategies. For example, I've got a list at my front door of what to grab in case of a fire.

Susan: Of course. That's a good thing to do. I'd always been in the house when we made the decision to evacuate in previous fires and was able to go through our possessions. It's usually hours before you make the decision and think through what toys should I take for the kids. Send the kids to a relative out of the line of fire. I think those things; they're good to do.

There's one other thing I'd say that in the event that your home and possessions are totally destroyed in a bushfire: use it as an opportunity to do something you would otherwise not have had the chance to do. **Every day we wake up in our house and we go, Oh my goodness, this is a wonderful home to live in. We've built something we would never have been able to build had the house not burned down.** We wouldn't have been able to finance it. We just wouldn't have done that. We're really grateful that out of something terrible, we've actually built something we just adore living in.

Karon: Gratitude for what you do have?

Susan: I think so. **There's something rather cleansing about losing everything and having to start again.** You don't have those emotional attachments to a piece of furniture or those obligations where you go, "Oh, well, that was the sideboard that Mum gave me and, we really should keep that." To have a fresh start is a bit of a gift.

Karon: A fresh start is always a gift, isn't it?

Susan: Yes.

Key Concepts

The loss of a home is considered a disaster and can take years to recover from, physically, emotionally and mentally. There is grief over the lost possessions, a loved home, the community you are used to and it continues for a number of years. Waves of grief are to be expected but you never know when they will hit. If there are lives lost it is complicated by the grief of losing a loved person which is very challenging in itself, let alone attending to accommodation issues and rebuilding a home.

Underinsured homes become a complicating factor for many losing their home to fire where you may find you can't afford to rebuild. This was the case for many in these fires.

Things that helped Susan's recovery:

1. When her friend talked of the death of his son it helped Susan to put into perspective that it was a house that was gone but not the loss of a loved family member.

2. Being able to stay at the home of her parents immediately brought familiarity as opposed to staying in an evacuation centre or unfamiliar accommodation.

3. Focussing on work as she found in shock her world shrank and she could only focus on one thing at a time.

4. Being comfortable saying to people, "Oh, look, I cry a bit now; I'm okay but I cry."

5. Recognising the process of recovering means you're never the same person.

6. "Ensure you can rebuild or relocate and you have the wherewithal to move on from the event." Not being underinsured is so important when disaster strikes.

7. Seeing the rebuilding of their home and life as an opportunity for a fresh start.

8. Susan has championed the needs of people following bushfires in her position as MP. She continued to do so following the bushfires all over Australia in the summer of 2019–20. This is a legacy of her traumatic loss of her home.

The Evacuation Centre

I was fortunate to interview **Heather Gwilliam, Regional Coordinator and Team Leader, Disaster Recovery Team, Anglicare.** She was able to tell me about the logistics of creating and running an evacuation centre, as it was her responsibility following the fires that day. Along with Red Cross, the Salvation Army and others their role is to assist the Department of Community Services in running evacuation centres in a natural disaster to provide a safe place to stay, food and water and information.

Heather described arriving in Springwood to see approximately 1000 people milling on the bowling greens outside the Springwood Sports Club that afternoon. The club was designated to be the evacuation centre. The club ceased trading and its kitchen was opened to provide food. There was a lot of confusion as to who had lost their homes. People were registered and interviewed by the Department of Community Housing and encouraged to stay with relatives and friends if possible. Some 110 people stayed on the first night. People were sitting with neighbours and looking out for each other. The Rural Fire Service provided a camp bed, a pillow and sleeping bag for each person. Evacuee's wanted to watch the TV news to see what had happened. Many had been at work and had no idea of the events of the day. Where ever possible temporary accommodation was provided in a motel, guest house or B&B for the evacuees.

There were pre-schoolers from a local pre-school whose parents couldn't get to them and the pre-school Director and her daughter stayed with them in the club. They were given the Board room for privacy.

The principal of Thomas Aquinas School walked the children out to safety only to find his house had been burnt down.

Mobile telephone towers went down. People forgot to bring mobile-chargers or they were lost in their burnt homes.

Doctors came to the centre after work to write scripts for people who had lost their medications in the fires. Heather had to take a huge number of scripts to the late hours pharmacy to have them made up and she arrived back around midnight to give all the medications out.

By midday the day after the fires there were no rental properties available locally as they had all been taken by those who had lost their homes. Food was provided all day, buffet style, to whoever needed it including the volunteers. Electric power was out for a week so those with homes would also come to the club for meals.

There were lots of animals in the evacuation centre. Heather said, "The animals were amazing, they didn't fight or make any trouble." The RSPCA and the NSW Agricultural Department came on the second day and set up cages and enclosures for the animals. Local vets also took some of the animals for treatment.

The fires continued to burn through the valleys for the next few days. Some people were evacuated four times in three days.

The first reaction people have is 'Thank god we got out and we're alive.' Parents are relieved when reunited with children. There was almost elation. Some were shaking and in shock. Some needed hugs. Some people looked fine. Some were crying and upset. Some angry. Many worried. Very few people were reported missing and all were quickly found. "I remember Susan Templeman had been trying to support others but day three or four she was hit with the reality and became tearful needing a hug herself," said Heather.

There was lots of community support. However, as Susan pointed out donations of money are best following disasters.

Unfortunately, people turned up with metal detectors looking for jewellery in the destroyed homes, so police had to set up and monitor a roadblock, to only allow locals in to prevent theft. You see the best and the worst of humans in disasters. Norman Lindsay's Art Gallery had guards and firefighters camping there to protect the precious art.

Day three, four, five or six is when the reality hits and then it's a nightmare. Adding to that were arguments with insurance companies and distress over authorities painting homes with asbestos, blue. Tension between neighbours exacerbated the emotional response. People often have other stressors in their lives before the fires that can complicate their recovery.

Reports of domestic violence increases after traumatic events like these as a result of people being stressed and feeling they have no control over their lives. It's a factor to be considered by those assisting recovery.

Fortunately, there were no lives lost in these fires but over 200 homes were lost, affecting over 1000 people. The support agencies continued their work for at least 12 months after the fires.

Heather Gwilliam OAM CF

Chapter 8

Greg Alexander

"I know the feeling of longing desperately for everything to be as it was before and the slow awakening to the fact that you are forever changed and life can never be the same again. That becomes a turning point where you can start to move forward."

Karon Coombs

GREGORY PETER STEPHAN 'BRANDY' ALEXANDER Biography

Famous Australian Rugby League Player

Penrith's first 'home-grown' Test player, Greg Alexander displayed a unique ability during his career to score and set up tries. Fast, with an elusive step and swerve, 'Brandy' Alexander was also a great tactical kicker, a confident goal-kicker and an excellent cover-defender. A star schoolboy footballer, Alexander made a stunning impact with the Panthers in 1984. He was duly named 'Dally M' Rookie of the Year, and in 1985, 'Dally M' Player of the Year. In 1986 Alexander was a late call-up to the 1986 Kangaroos squad. Played City Origin, State of Origin and for Australia. Captained Penrith's first Premiership win in 1991.

In 1997 his brilliant form earned him an NSW halfback's jersey in the Super League Tri-Series but a foot injury saw him miss the remainder of the season. While his final three seasons with the Panthers were injury-ridden Alexander retired in 1999 as only the second player in history (after Terry Lamb) to score 100 tries and 1000 pts for the one club. Alexander has since established a career as a skills coach with the Panthers and a sports commentator with Radio 2UE and Fox Sports. His autobiography is *Five Star Brandy* (1991).

Left to Right – Ben, Greg and Peter Alexander

He has been a Panthers' Director for 16 years and involved with Rugby League in the Penrith area for 40 years. He is considered a gentleman of the sports world and was inducted into the Penrith Hall of Fame. He is married to Tanya and they have four sons. The car crash death of his brother Ben had a life-changing impact on him.

The Interview

Karon: Greg, as a child, did you ever imagine having a successful career as a footballer?

Greg: I grew up in Cranebrook, Western Sydney, NSW. We lived on five acres and I remember my dad in the backyard, talking to a man while pointing at me (I must've been six or seven), he said "That boy will play for Australia". That stuck with me, I think I fell in love with league. I loved playing. I don't know whether it was a subconscious thing, but there were periods while growing up that I thought, I'm not good enough but I kept at it.

Karon: You were more than good enough. You played for Australia as well as Penrith Panthers. It looked like your younger brother; Ben was an exceptional player too.

Greg: Ben was a great player. Peter, my other brother, played for Penrith as well. Not first grade but he played lower grades. The three of us grew up playing football in the backyard. The year we won the comp, I think Ben played 18 first grade games. He was only 19 and was very good.

Karon: The newspaper described Ben as a rising star.

Greg: He started very young. Like Ben, I didn't play much reserve grade, I sort of came from school to first grade. I was 18 when we started playing, the year I debuted. Ben was playing reserve grade at 16. He was quicker than I was. He was a rising star, that's for sure.

Karon: Can you describe Ben for me?

Greg: For a young person, he had a unique personality. Around our family, Ben was always the wisecrack. He was the personality in the family. Wherever there was a discussion around the dinner table, most of the time it wasn't politically correct, because there were five of us and we normally had others around when we got older. Ben was the personality and he had that ability to pull people together of all ages. In the football team, Ben was the baby, but he was the life and the personality. He had the ability to attract attention and be the life. He wasn't a show-off, but he was quick and had that ability to attract attention. My other brother, Pete, and I were quiet, pretty reserved. Ben wasn't reserved.

Karon: Ben was gregarious?

Greg: Exactly. He was. He had the confidence to put himself into conversations with people, whereas I would stand back and watch. Even though he was seven years younger than me, Ben was someone that I thought, 'Wow, look at this kid, he's remarkable.' But that's only a small percentage of his personality. Ben was such a kind-hearted, big hearted person that would do anything for anyone. There were a whole range of things. Even though Ben was gregarious, he was a beautiful boy.

Karon: He was tragically killed in a car accident on the 25 June 1992. If you could go back to the 48 hours before Ben's accident, what would you say to him?

Greg: Don't drink and drive. That's what I'd say. It's a funny thing, isn't it, when you look back on situations like that. For a while, I sort of felt "God, why couldn't I do anything to stop it?" Panthers played footy that day. I didn't play. I was injured at the time because I hurt my knee weeks before. We had our blazer presentation for our 1991 Premiership win that night. We were at Panthers Events Centre and my Dad was with us. Dad didn't live with us, but I'd gone and picked him up for the day and brought him out. He came to the presentation and I remember Ben and a few of the younger boys wanting to go to a nightclub. I said to him, don't go anywhere. Dad's here. Stay here. For whatever reason, whether I was with Dad or whatever, I didn't realise Ben had left until someone came back an hour later and said there had been an accident. I was still at Panthers, but I didn't know any details. There was a lot of thought about why I wasn't stronger in saying to Ben, "Do not leave." I went to the accident with a friend. They wouldn't tell me what happened but I knew it wasn't good.

Karon: Was Ben still in the car when you arrived at the accident?

Greg: Yes. If only I had convinced Ben to stay with me and the boys.

If only. I didn't know straight away that he was dead. I can't remember who told me. The accident is a blur. I can't remember exactly what went on there.

Karon: You no doubt went into shock when you arrived at the scene and saw what had happened.

Greg: Probably. It wasn't good.

Karon: Did you beat up on yourself about not stopping Ben from leaving Panthers?

Greg: I probably didn't that much but I was so distraught, I didn't know what I was thinking. I probably did think that but it wasn't an overriding emotion that I should have done more.

Karon: More like passing thoughts.

Greg: Yes. It didn't stick with me. It wasn't something that I thought, I should have done more. I'm realistic.

Karon: Ben was 20, he would've done what he wanted anyway.

Greg: That's right.

Karon: I understand that's the message you are trying to get out to young men now. Don't drink and drive.

Greg: It's a pretty simple one, isn't it? **Don't drink and drive. Because we know, there are a whole lot of other things that come out of it. The effect of what you do on the people that have to live with your decision.**

Karon: Absolutely. I understand it's not easy talking about Ben's death, but I would appreciate it if you could explain the knock-on effect for the family after a sudden death, because it's the people left behind that suffer.

Greg: **Well, I think everyone's different. It affects everyone differently. I can only talk about what happened to us. We didn't fall apart as a family, it shattered us.** There's a lot of emotion that goes on particularly early, but how it affected us was I wanted to get out of Penrith. I had only recently left home, I was 26. Ben was living in my house; he'd moved in with me. A year, two years later, I left Penrith and went to New Zealand and played for the Warriors football club. My brother-in-law, Mark Geyer, and Megan, my sister, married. They left to live in Perth. Mum went to Perth with Megan because she had started to have kids and start a family. My other sister Linda went to Perth with her boyfriend, soon to be husband. My brother, Peter, worked for a while and came and lived with me for a year in New Zealand. The family split up. It affected the club. **It had a huge, massive impact on the Panthers and what happened in the club over the next five or six years.**

Karon: Were you getting away from all the media attention?

Greg: No, not really. I lost the passion to play football. That's how it affected me. I don't know why, but I did. I needed something new, something that's a new challenge to try and spark me. I was only 28 or 29. It was more about me not trying to fail in something new. I found it hard living in Penrith. I left because I needed something new.

Karon: A lot of people don't realise when a death is sudden and unexpected that somebody has to tell the family the news. Who was that in Ben's case?

Greg: A teammate, Craig Izzard, who was a policeman at the time, he went around to our house on official duty and told Mum.

In his book, Rugby League Rebel, *Mark Geyer describes being asleep that night in Ben's mum's house and being woken by a piercing scream. "I sat bolt upright in bed... with a sense something was terribly wrong." Then discovering Ben was dead, he stated, "I was shattered. I didn't know what to do. I felt like punching a wall and screaming...It was devastating."*

Karon: Usually somebody has to identify the body. Who had to do that in Ben's case?

Greg: I don't know. I can't remember. It wasn't me.

Karon: Greg, were you offered support? Were you and your family offered counselling?

Greg: I think…did we have a pastor at the club? I don't know. We weren't offered support. No, not professional help. No, I don't think we even thought about it or anyone thought about it, back in 1992. Things have changed, I'm sure the welfare of players would be addressed today. There are associations now. I'm sure that'd be completely different now. Our support system was your teammates or your coach. Nothing organised and I'm not being critical. I'm saying… That was the way of the world back then.

Karon: Did it help going to New Zealand for a couple of years?

Greg: Absolutely. It was the beginning of the Auckland Warriors who started in 1995. I went there mid-September 94 with my girlfriend who I married two years later. It was almost like starting a new life and what I needed. That helped me.

Karon: Helped your recovery?

Greg: Absolutely. I loved it because we lived right in the city, it was different for me, compared with growing up in Penrith. It was completely new. New team, new teammates, new living, new country. I think it was good and I certainly don't regret doing it. I would love to have stayed at Penrith Panthers forever, but it didn't work out that way. New Zealand provided the fresh start and the people in New Zealand, the Warriors, in those fledgling years were fantastic. We had between nine and ten players who had never played ARL or first grade football before. There were no egos and it was a great experience for me because these blokes wanted to learn what it was like to play in the NRL. In the end it was Royce Simmons, who I had played alongside at the Panthers, brought me home after taking over as coach. I ended up coming back to Penrith and playing for another three years. That was good because I came back, married and started a family. That was different too. That experience of living away from Penrith took me to the northern beaches of Sydney, not long after starting to have a family. I think having my own family was the other big healing period of my getting over the death of Ben. Having my own four boys was definitely a big thing. A different focus. Life changes.

Karon: New life.

Greg: I'm lucky that I had the chance to do that, to start again, to help me get over the grief. I completely lost my passion for rugby league and I don't know why that happened.

Karon: I think because all your energy is going into grieving and there's not much energy left over for anything else.

Greg: Footy is a hard game to play when it's not your priority. I really struggled.

Karon: How did it affect your dad?

Greg: Well, Dad was a no-nonsense sort of bloke. My mum and dad split up when I was ten, Ben was two or three years old. Ben didn't grow up with Dad. Dad was not a huge part of our lives; he was a bigger part of my life because I was older. Obviously, his son died, and Dad was at the Panthers too with me. I don't know what sort of impact it made on Dad. Obviously, it hurt him, but he's pretty much a 'get on with it' guy.

Karon: Could I ask how it affected your mum?

Greg: It destroyed Mum. Mum raised us. For a long time, Mum was, I don't know how to explain it, how to describe what it did, to say that it broke her. Absolutely! God, I wouldn't even know how to put it, but it changed her. **It's like someone chipped away at her soul and she was sad.** People say time heals. Even though it's time, it's always there and life goes on and on and on and on and then, **it's not as if it happens one day where you think you're good. It's such a gradual thing that you don't even notice it happening to you. You know, 25 years down the track and I still get emotional.**

Karon: Do you find anniversary times difficult?

Greg: I do. I find it's hard to explain how you feel. It's a sad period.

Karon: Every year?

Greg: Yeah, every year. I found early, that Ben's birthday and Christmases were even more difficult periods.

Karon: I guess it is difficult thinking your sons grew up without an uncle.

Greg: That's true. Especially when they were younger, when it was all new and I thought I would have loved to have Ben involved in their lives because of the sort of person he was. It's a great shame that they missed out on Uncle Ben, who would've been the absolute best. I'm sure they would've loved him so much.

Karon: It sounds like he would've been a fun uncle.

Greg: He was a fun boy. I often wonder what he would have been like. He would be 48 now. It's funny talking about him like that.

Karon: You said your eldest sons are 17 and 19. What happens to you when they go out for a night out?

Greg: I worry. The 19-year-old doesn't go out much, bit of a homebody. But he does go out with his friends. He went to school at Kirribilli, so his friends are all Sydney boys. If they do go out, they'll go into town. I'm still waiting for the 17-year-old to be 18 and going out. It's a worry.

Karon: You wouldn't be able to not worry.

Greg: No, that's right. I don't worry about my boys as much as I worry about other people getting in cars and driving. My boys might be getting in that car, but they're smart boys.

Karon: I guess you've warned them.

Greg: They've had a good education about what can happen. It's indiscriminate. Things happen quickly and it can be one decision that can have an impact on them. They know about loss and the effect of poor decisions.

Karon: Would you have any advice for people who experienced a sudden and unexpected death? About how to cope, how to survive?

Greg: You know what, I don't know if anyone could give advice. Even professionals that counsel people about loss, I guess there's some guidelines **but everyone's so different and everyone feels and reacts to loss differently. I was a miserable failure at it. I didn't cope with it. It affected everything I did, and affected me for years.** I certainly have no advice because looking back on it now; I didn't handle it well at all. But I don't regret that. It was my way of handling it. It was me getting through that period, waking up the next day and trying to get through it. It was like that for years. But of course, life carried on. It was a bit robotic and a bit meaningless and a bit distracted.

Karon: Your wife must be wonderful, because she's coped with your grief reactions.

Greg: My wife Tan, went to school with Ben and they were friends. She was best friends with my youngest sister, Linda, and they all went to school together. They were only a year below each other. I wasn't going out with Tan when the accident happened.

Karon: Maybe the fact that she knew him so well helped her understand your reactions?

Greg: Probably did. I'm sure it did. Absolutely!

Karon: That's lovely to hear.

Greg: It's a good story [smiling].

Karon: Can you explain what the Knock-on Effect campaign is?

Greg: Well, it's a campaign aimed at not just young people but everyone who makes decisions when they're driving. Whether they decide to drive, what they do in all the decisions they make, not drunk driving but mobile phone use in cars. Distractions in cars. I try to relate my story to how it can affect someone and what affect it still is having 25 years down the track. I'm not unusual. Everyone that loses someone that's close to them lives with that for the rest of their lives to a varying degree of how it affects them.

Karon: You change forever?

Greg: **That's right. The Knock-on campaign is about that, about what effect a poor decision surrounding driving a motor vehicle can have and who suffers. Think about things before you do them and think about being responsible and accountable for your own actions. Your own actions do affect everyone you know.**

Karon: Is the campaign being taken into schools?

Greg: Yes, yes, yes. It's been taken into schools and the video that I made with Roads New South Wales is being shown in schools. Through State of Origin, our New South Wales players went to schools through one of our camps and spoke to the children. It's all through the schools.

Karon: That's a great legacy, isn't it?

Greg: Yeah, it is. **I did say through the making of the video that if I had my choice, I didn't want Ben's accident, I didn't want it to be a lesson. I didn't want him to become a lesson for everyone. But if I can tell my story and it has a positive effect on someone then it's worthwhile.**

The Coroner's Report mentioned a blood alcohol reading of 0.14, almost three times the limit and Ben was not wearing a seatbelt when he hit a power pole. The ambulance had reached the scene in four minutes but that was too late for Ben.

Bernard Carlon, Centre for Road Safety and Maritime Safety Director says, "Every 41 minutes someone is killed or seriously injured on NSW roads… We are asking everyone, drivers, riders, passengers and pedestrians – to think about the consequences of their actions."

Brad Fittler, who is also involved in the campaign and was a team mate of both Greg and Ben, added: "Too many people are dying and it's having a devastating 'knock-on-effect' on families and local communities."

Key Concepts

The sudden and unexpected death of someone you love has a huge impact on your life for years to come, as Greg experienced. It impacts the whole family as well as those around them. In this case the Panthers football family were also devastated for a long time. Greg makes a good point when he says he still gets emotional now, 25 years down the track because there is always a little grief for the rest of your life but people learn to live with it and manage it.

Things that helped Greg's recovery:

1. Having a supportive wife in Tanya.

2. Having someone who is not a member of the family to tell the family members what had happened. The person delivering the news is often seen as partly causing it because before they knew the news, they were alright. That's an example of, 'Don't shoot the messenger'.

3. Moving to a new location and the stimulation of new work as a footballer.

4. Having a family of his own meant he needed to be responsible for his children and focus on them.

5. Using the support system of the team members and coach.

6. Talking about his grief journey.

7. Knowing that each birthday and death day anniversaries and Christmas will be challenging and preparing for them helps.

8. Knowing time does not heal everything, but grief becomes more manageable as the years pass as you become familiar with the territory.

9. Being involved with the Knock-on Effect Campaign as a legacy created some positivity and gave meaning to Ben's death.

Chapter 9

Brett Kakoschke

"*Look to fix your problems with love, compassion, patience and virtue.*

Every energy, every emotion, every experience has its place in the grand scheme of things. Knowing this will make your journey along life's often difficult road a little more bearable."

Ezio De Angelis (Medium)

BRETT KAKOSCHKE Biography

Business owner

Brett currently resides in the Blue Mountains with his wife of 11 years, Rebecca, and two beautiful daughters, Mikayla, four, and Bella, two. His girls are the centre of his world and keep him very busy!

Born in Adelaide, Brett has grown up in a variety of towns and cities, moving from South Australia to Bundaberg, Queensland.

Growing up Brett was always part of family businesses, which led to a varied working life.

After leaving school, he spent eight years in the army. He then moved on to be self-employed in a number of businesses, including trucking and landscaping. This was followed by a career as a chef for eight years, including being head chef at a successful restaurant.

During this time Brett also trained as a reiki master. He taught reiki, worked with clients doing past life regressions and was assistant coordinator at Blaxland Spiritual Centre.

Brett currently runs his own business doing building maintenance and has done so for the last 12 years.

The Interview

Karon: Brett, thank you for being willing to share your story. I'm fascinated to hear of your near-death experience (NDE).

Brett: Mine's not near death, it's actual death because I died. When your heart stops, you're dead. When your body shuts down, it's over. **I had a full visit to the other side.**

Karon: Can you start by telling me a little bit about your life before you had that experience?

Brett: Over the years, I knew there was something wrong with my body. I served in the army and was physically fit and played competitive sports. Doctors did tests and couldn't find the cause. When I did the heart stress test, I was told I would break the machine. I was told nothing was wrong with me and it was in my head. There were a few times when I became faint and passed out. One time I blacked out while driving. I lost my vision but was conscious and still able to drive. My vision returned before I hit a guardrail. Another time I passed out and fell over and split my chin. Another time was like a Mandala. I passed out and there were colours all around me. When I visited the doctor, nothing could be found.

One day, when I came home from work, I was feeling bad. I lay on the floor and told my wife, "I can feel my body shutting down." About half an hour later I was sitting in the office doing paperwork and I called her and said, "I can feel it," because I knew when the attacks were coming. I could feel it getting tingly and the blacks starting to come. Next thing I was gone. Dead. For me, it wasn't Pearly Gates and God. There were two spirits there holding my hands out and talking to me. For a long time afterwards, I was upset that I couldn't recall what they were saying to me because we were having a conversation. To this day I still can't remember anything said.

Some people believe, when you die, you either go to hell or heaven or nothing. The feelings that I experienced there would make this place feel more like hell than anything else because of the stress, the worry and the concerns. Everything you have here is gone. I remember all the colours which looked like the Hubble space pictures of Orion. All those amazing colours and the gas clouds. That's what it felt like. I was somewhere like that. I didn't have a white tunnel; I didn't have Pearly Gates. **There were two people there waiting for me, two beings. That must be the message to me that someone's always there for everybody. The colour really stuck with me for a long time. Colour doesn't exist here compared to the colour that I saw on that side. An amazing place with absolute contentment and a feeling of everything gone.** Knowing when you die, there's nothing to be scared of. There's full contentment, and total freedom. Everything that we have from this world is lifted and disappears. You have no feeling, no stress, no concerns, and no worries. Mine was short-term, maybe if it had been longer, I'd know what you think about the people and things you have left behind. I don't know how that works. **But for that first period, you're taken out of your body and everything from this world is left behind. You're weightless, no pain, no fear, totally content.** When I came to, my wife thought I was playing a joke on her because she said she had never seen me so happy or content. I came to with a massive smile on my face.

About a minute after I came to, all the colour drained out of me. I went grey and felt sick. I looked at her and said, "What's wrong? What are you doing?" I had no idea that I had died, and my heart had stopped. My wife frantically phoned 000 to get an ambulance. She couldn't get through. There was nothing she could do. She said I was dead in the chair. It would have been one to two minutes. That's when I knew I was somewhere else because I knew exactly what happened that time. I knew I was with two other beings, two people, and the colours and everything made this world look black and white.

I believe there was a message for me in this experience. I was involved in teaching reiki and doing past life meditations for people. I believe we go to somewhere else in spirit. This time I received confirmation and I was with two other beings, wherever I was. There were two figures I could not see. More like an energy, and I was supposed to realise it was the colour and knowing I was actually somewhere.

Karon: I've sometimes heard of people saying they were sorry they came back because where they'd been was so beautiful.

Brett: I've always said ever since that day, I can totally understand why people don't want to come back. I said that to my wife and other people I've spoken to. I can totally see people would have said that they've fought, "No, no. I don't want to go back." I was shoved back.

Karon: You were pushed back?

Brett: Mine was quick because my heart stopped, then bang, the heart kicked back in, and suddenly, I woke up quickly. I don't think I was given a choice whether I wanted to stay or not. I think maybe other people who have had bad accidents and their body is beyond repair, maybe they have more of a choice. **Within the next day or two I felt so blessed and privileged that I could feel and experience what was on the other side.**

No matter what it is, I'm not religious so I do not call it heaven. I don't believe in a single God or anything like that, and it didn't confirm religion for me. In a sense, it probably makes me more confused knowing that I have been on the other side and it didn't answer those questions. It didn't slap me in the face and say, "You were wrong. I'm God. I'm here. You've been wrong all this time not believing in me." I did not have a religious-type experience. Spiritual, yes, because there were two spirits or beings to greet me, or there to push me back saying, "You've got someone; you've got more to do." It was such a privileged experience. I felt brilliance and it's something you can't experience while you're alive on earth. That was the proof for me, to have that and then come back and know.

I felt really off and rang my local doctor who advised me to attend his surgery immediately. After telling him what happened, I had a heart monitor attached. A day later the doctor advised me that my heart had stopped. I had a full heart blockage. My heart was stopping, shutting down totally. Within a week I had a pacemaker, so I didn't drop off again.

Karon: What does the pacemaker do?

Brett: If my heart stops, it kicks it back up again. If it gets down to a certain rate, it kicks it in. They say my heart would have stopped a lot of times during my sleep. I realised a lot of times where I'd woken up in sweats, because that's what happened after I came back. I mean I'd get all grey and sweaty and feel terrible. My heart slows and would get so relaxed, it would turn off, and stop, and shut my whole body down. It was happening a lot.

Karon: Are you're perfectly okay now, with the pacemaker? No more blackouts?

Brett: No more blackouts. I don't have any medication or anything. I have six-monthly check-ups on my pacemaker. They put a machine on and they check it to make sure everything's fine.

Karon: How has your experience impacted your life since then? Has it influenced the way you look at life?

Brett: It didn't change me in the sense that, I have to live my life totally differently. That's probably more since I had my little girls. I don't think it changed me straightaway in the sense of, "Oh, I have to do this," or, "I'm going to preach this," or, "I'm going to let other people know." There was a couple of instances that I thought my experience was to help those people I've spoken to.

One time the lady, who was doing the heart monitor check, and had not seen me before, asked what happened because I was still young. I told her and she questioned me, "Oh, you actually think you died and went on the other side?" Then she asked me what I saw and what I experienced. She got a bit emotional, and then was really, happy and thanked me for telling her because, she had lost her daughter six months previously and she said that made her feel a lot more comfortable knowing her daughter was in a nice place. There's been a couple of times I've spoken to people and they seemed to have the response, **"Oh, wow. Oh, that's good," and their fear goes. They don't have as much worry, their concern of their loved one's suffering seems to go because if they really believe you, you can see it drain from their life.**

I used to do reiki and past life regression with people. I have had lots of experiences where I've sat with people and they talked of loss and death in their lives. That's why they end up going to someone who does the spiritual work to see if they can connect with the spirit of their lost loved ones. The whole experience for me was a validation of what I'd done, because my experience happened when I started my business, and I didn't have time to do spirit work anymore. Spiritual work is about working with the people and you're giving a gift back.

Because of my experience, I understand a lot more of what people are seeing and experiencing during meditations and their past life regressions. In terms of my life, I thought about writing about it, talking to people about it. Then I always come back to, if people ask about it, they're the ones that are going to listen and they're the ones that are going to believe what I say and benefit. I've spoken to people from different cultures. **One thing I noticed is it's universal. It doesn't matter what religion they're from, everyone wants to know about what happens after death and where they're going to.** I suppose the same thing probably happens to all of us no matter what our beliefs are. I choose to veer on the side of knowing what I experienced. I know what I see is real. A lot of things I have seen in life, most people will not even believe.

Karon: What kind of things are they?

Brett: Very young exposed to the spirit.

Karon: You could see spirits?

Brett: Almost all my life. Connections to spirit. Not that I remembered until I was in my thirties, when I started getting involved in the spiritual circle and meditation. Then I realised that it wasn't imagination, it was real. As a kid, my parents would always tell me I was making it up or it was my imagination.

I don't think I was ever scared of death because I've had a few close calls and experiences. Lots of spiritual experiences. An extra-terrestrial one with beings from somewhere else. I don't know what that is, I can't explain. But I connected with and got a lot more belief when I started doing past life regressions for people, which is mainly about them going back and healing to move forward. One of my clients was an ex-policeman. His wife, through the Blaxland Spiritual Centre, found out about me, and sent him to me as he was in and out of hospital, suicidal and very black with depression because of what he'd experienced in his work. He was a sceptic because he said he did not believe in spiritual healing. What I do, is not about what happens for me. The experience is for them. What I do is help the person relax and give them a place where their spirit would come through. Whatever messages they get is for them. I try and help them interpret whatever their feelings are.

During the ex-policeman's healing, I could feel two spirits. Initially, I didn't know if it was a male or a female. I couldn't tell, which was unusual. He came through with a lot of guilt and resentment because I can feel the pain. He had medical issues with his hip his whole life and the doctors couldn't fix it after the accident. They said, "This is a disability you now have." He felt that lift and go while we were doing the healing session. The whole time, I was getting resentment, guilt with this male and female present. At the end of the session, we talked about it and he told me what had happened to him. He said, "I was in an accident during a car chase and an innocent couple got killed. My life changed after that." I said, "Well, there's your male and your female." The whole time they were saying, through me "We don't hold you responsible. Don't feel guilty for what happened. We know it wasn't your fault."

That released everything that the ex-policeman had been holding onto all those years, all his pain, everything disappeared from that day and he left a different man. I found out because his wife came up to me a couple of weeks later. She ran up in tears and gave me hug and said, "Thank you for giving me my husband back." I do it for free to get that fulfillment. I haven't had time to practice since establishing my business, but it's something I would love to continue to do. I'm raising a family and that work is very hard to do from there, because I don't accept payment.

Karon: Maybe later in your life? The ex-policeman could not have got that message from any other form of counselling. Nobody could have told him, "You don't have to hold that guilt. We don't hold you responsible." That's lovely healing work.

Brett: No. It's only from the spirit, those on the other side coming back to heal and release him and letting him know they didn't feel bad and that they knew it wasn't his fault. During his regression back, because it's not always past life, that was a current life regression but it took him back to that time earlier in this life so he could heal.

Some go right back into different centuries. He was a total nonbeliever beforehand. He said, "You've got a cliff face on rocks here." You can't see that from where my meditation room used to be at the back of the property. He said, "I can see an alien, creatures on here, at this property. I can see them running around the rocks." To me, it was strange that someone had seen that. He explained to me what he saw. I said, "Well, I have seen them here once before, myself." I thought it might have been my imagination from watching movies like *Stargate* because it was something like that showing in one of his movies. Lots of experiences like that with people, and a broad spectrum of people's lives. You're basically stepping in their life and their experience and I feel everything and that's how I get the message.

I didn't have people sitting there like you and me across the table going, "Tell them this, tell them that." That's not how it works with me. You might get people like John Edwards, the psychic medium, who does readings on his TV show called *Crossing Over*, who would say, "They're telling me this, their giving me that." Mine wasn't like that. Mine was feeling their energy and trying to interpret the message, whatever was being given to them. I didn't see the people. I would know when I was connecting with people, I was giving the message to, because they will feel and know that it's for them. It means nothing to me because I'm a vessel to help them out.

Karon: Wow. What an amazing ability.

Brett: It always shocked me. I didn't know until later what it was and what was happening. The past life thing is something I'd been interested in, but I didn't know that was going to happen when I started doing reiki. That was not what I thought I was going to be doing with the healing sessions for people. It happened. One of my first ever clients is where it started. From that day, whenever I did a session, it seemed to keep happening. I went with it, realising that's what I'm supposed to help people with. It's not my choice, it's spirit. The past is probably the most important thing in people's lives. We can't move on unless we heal the past because it's holding us back. What I learned is, you can go back, heal and then move on in this life.

Karon: That certainly seems to be true and your experience tells us the other side of death is a beautiful experience. I've seen that in my palliative care work. In the last few weeks of life. People have one foot in this world and one foot in the next world and they seem to easily pass between the worlds. If you listen without judgment, they'll tell you that they met people they knew, or they met angels, but they feel peaceful about dying after they've had that experience. I believe in an afterworld simply because I've heard from so many people close to death telling me the things they've seen of the next world.

Brett: That's, obviously, preparation for death.

Karon: I believe it is.

Brett: I believe there's someone there waiting for us, because I experienced two beings waiting for me. Then quickly, not your time. There were a few times, where I basically should have been dead. I was hit by car when I was 16 years old and that was one of my first full out of body experiences. I didn't know what had happened until later in life, when I was meditating, and I thought back on that experience. I was hit so hard I was knocked out of my body. I remember running back down the road to the car that hit me because they'd stopped, and my friends were there. Another mate who was riding with me didn't get hit. He was standing there talking. I could hear them talking and I'm running back down the road to these people talking to me, but they're looking down at me on the road, talking to me. I ran back, back into my body and then I woke and was fine. I didn't receive an injury. Hit at 80 kilometres an hour by a four-wheel drive. Full-on side impact on a pushbike with only a little bruising. There was a big bull-bar on it as well.

Karon: On a pushbike? That's incredible.

Brett: I could feel myself rolling down the bitumen and that's what surprised me because there were no grazes, nothing. My spirit and my energy being, were knocked out of my physical body, rolling down the road. My physical body was still back at the car. It hadn't been scraped on the bitumen. They were saying to me, "You're all right. You're all right." I ran back to them. I went from the scene and I was sick that night with concussion maybe. I was throwing up and very sick, but we had been drinking. That one saved me too, being so relaxed, I was able to be knocked out of my body.

They say drunk people are always the ones that survive accidents because their bodies are relaxed. But that was a very early out of body experience and back in. I probably shouldn't have survived that one, without a scratch.

Karon: Bizarre.

Brett: You're right. It makes you wonder when things like this happen you ask, "Well, what makes me special? Why am I cheating death and getting away with it and coming back?"

Karon: We all ask, "Why me?" don't we when unusual things happen.

Brett: Normally it's the other way, "Why is something bad happening? Why does this keep happening to me?" Whereas if it's the other side you go, "Well, why am I being so blessed? Why am I being given the gift to stay? Why am I still alive and able to come back? Is it a gift or...? Or no, it's better over there now." But probably not for my own reasons now. Lucky, I have my two girls. They're the important things in life. I'm very privileged for the experience. I wondered a lot what I could do with it. It's one of those things you want to tell people, "Oh, everything's okay when you die."

When people need that help or they need answers for something, they'll be guided to the right person that will give it to them. That's how I look at it with spiritual workers and people that do spiritual readings. I think a lot of them get a bit stuck trying to interpret things in their own language where it's not what it's about. You've got to give that message as you receive it. Not try and explain that message to someone because then you're putting it in your terms. Sometimes it's one word or thing you say, and everything clicks for them. They seem to understand their whole issue, or problem.

Like the experience with the lady whose daughter had died. She questioned me; I would never have told her about what happened except, she was doing the testing on my heart monitor and asked me about it. All of a sudden, she's now got an experience where she feels a lot better about her daughter's passing. She said, "I am much happier now." I could see it in her. It totally changed her on the spot. It gave her hope.

I'm not making money off it. I haven't written a book. I'm not trying to sell my story. If you want to hear it, I'll tell you it, but you do what you want with it. You can only believe what you experience. That's why I don't try and teach my girls anything. When they're old enough they can look for answers and search for things. They are already experiencing spirits, ghosts, visitors. They come and tell us all the time what's happened in detailed experiences at four and two years and have done so for a couple of years. My wife and I don't try to discourage them. Let them experience what they see. Because not only like you experienced with palliative care, spirits are waiting and ready to help. I believe there are a lot of children in spirit around playing with the kids.

You can see it with little babies. They're sitting on the floor and talking and jabbering away to the spirits we can't see. They are talking and having conversations with people, playing with them. There's something going on and they haven't been turned off. We get turned off as children by parents saying, "You're making it up. It's not real, you're imagining things." Well, maybe not.

Karon: They call it imaginary friends, don't they? But maybe they're spirits.

Brett: I heard John Edwards speak about the same experience as a child. He was turned off because a teacher told him it's not real and then when he got older, he started to experience and use his gifts.

I've never had a real fear of death for some reason. I drowned very early. It was another near-death experience. I think I was five or six. We lived in a coastal town and I was playing in a boat. I used to put the anchor out and let the boats flow as the tide came in and out. We were jumping off the boats because we could touch the bottom. I couldn't swim and jumped off and it was too deep. I remember floating to the bottom. I remember total calm, golden sunshine coming through the water, all the bubbles around me and I stopped struggling. I was slowly, slowly sinking. Then I had a hand come out of the water and pull me back up and put me on the boat. I thought that was my grandfather for some reason all those years. But he was nowhere near where we lived. It was obviously a grandfatherly figure that I had seen but there was no one in that boat.

Karon: Oh, it wasn't a physical being that pulled you out of the water?

Brett: To me, it was. I saw the hand, I saw him pull me onto the boat, but there was no one at all. There was no one around on the boat with us kids at all. That story is like, "Okay. Was there actually someone there?" But then I met another girl a few years back when I was involved in the spiritual centre. She sat there and I was talking to her about that experience one night and we both choked up. Got this real energy all around us. We both had goose bumps. She said, "I had exactly the same experience when I was young." She was drowning as well. She had fallen and a hand came and pulled her out of the water, but she said, "No one was there." As I said, I've never had that fear of death. Then being in the military you see a lot. You think differently of death when you've been in the military. We always used to celebrate death, very hard, but it was a massive big party when someone was killed or whatever, you celebrated their life rather than people being sad and raving about it for a long time. I think it was a psychological thing, how they train you to get on and you're back at work the next day and you don't think about it as much.

I don't know whether it was what I experienced as a kid and having those experiences that I never had real fear of death. I don't have it now and I'll be a lot happier knowing when people go that they're alright. It's going to be fine. You're going to be very happy.

Karon: Has this experience led you to a point where, if you lose people you love, you think that it'll make it easier?

Brett: Definitely, knowing that there's going to be someone there for them. **It's never easy to lose a loved one, but I'll be a lot happier knowing there's someone on the other side to take care of them. Absolutely, a lot happier.** Mine was a short one. I don't know whether if I'd gone further, if I'd spent more time knowing the process. Knowing that feeling and knowing that there's obviously someone there for you, makes me a lot happier for them. Of course, you're still sad when you lose people.

Karon: Well, that has been absolutely fascinating. Thank you so much for sharing your experiences Brett.

Key Concepts

'There are two recent bestselling books by doctors, *Proof of Heaven* by Eben Alexander – who writes about a near-death experience (NDE) he had while in a week-long coma brought on by meningitis – and *To Heaven and Back*, by Mary C. Neal, who had her NDE while submerged in a river after a kayaking accident.

Western NDEs are the most studied. Many of these stories relate the sensation of floating up and viewing the scene around one's unconscious body; spending time in a beautiful, otherworldly realm; meeting spiritual beings (some call them angels) and a loving presence that some call God; encountering long-lost relatives or friends; recalling scenes from one's life; feeling a sense of connectedness to all creation as well as a sense of overwhelming, transcendent love; and finally being called, reluctantly, away from the magical realm and back into one's own body. Many NDErs report that their experience did not feel like a dream or a hallucination but was, as they often describe it, "more real than real life." They are profoundly changed afterward, and tend to have trouble fitting back into everyday life. Some embark on radical career shifts or leave their spouses.'

Extracted from a story by Gideon Lichfield in *The Atlantic* magazine.

https://www.theatlantic.com/magazine/archive/2015/04/the-science-of-near-death-experiences/386231/

Seeing a medium/spiritual worker can provide relief from worry about the loved one who died and what has happened to them. For example, as Brett said about the policeman, "That released everything that the ex-policeman had been holding onto all those years, all his pain, guilt, everything disappeared from that day and he left a different man."

Things that helped Brett's recovery:

1. Getting medical interventions to finally diagnose the issue with his heart and treatment for it in the form of a pacemaker.

2. Working out the meaning and message behind his experience and feeling grateful he had the experience.

3. After reflecting on his experience and wondering why he had it, he felt the meaning was to tell others of his experience who were worried about their loved ones who had died and seeing the peace they feel afterwards.

4. Knowing people will cross his path if they need to hear his message that someone's always there for everybody after death and it is a beautiful, peaceful experience.

Give sorrow words; the grief that does not speak.

Whispers the o'erfraught heart and bids it break.

Shakespeare – Macbeth

Twelve Concepts to Support You During Your Grief Journey

"If as a culture, we don't bear witness to grief, the burden of loss is placed entirely on the bereaved while the rest of us avert our eyes and wait for those in mourning to stop being sad, to let go, to move on, to cheer up. And if they don't – if they have loved too deeply, if they do wake each morning thinking I cannot continue to live – well then, we pathologise their pain; we call their suffering a disease. We do not help them; we tell them that they need to get help."

Cheryl Strayed

I too have experienced intense grief after the death of my son. I also developed post-traumatic stress disorder as a result of the terrifying experience where his life and mine hung in the balance; which definitely complicated my grief. I did not do grief and bereavement well at times, resorting to alcohol to numb the pain. This of course only delayed my bereavement. Grief sits waiting for an opportunity to pop out at the most unexpected times. My wish is for others to suffer less and be wise about their grief and so I have put together this list of reflections that have come from my experience and those of the people in each chapter of this book.

1. **Suffering is universal and part of the human condition. It is also transformative.**

    If you can accept this truth and realise each one of us will have grief visit at some time in our life, if not numerous times, you can stop fighting your grief and let it have its rightful place. Respect it as a natural season in your life following loss and allow it to wash over you so your healing journey can happen.

2. **Be grateful for the experience of feeling great love.**

Grief is the flipside of love. Recognise a life without love is a hollow life and to have received and given love is the most wonderful experience. Your pain in grief comes from having loved someone or something intensely. The pain you have is in direct proportion to the love you have.

3. **Accept that there will be unbearable days in your grieving and know they will pass.**

The place of healing grief requires all your strength, faith and resilience. It is a terrifying place at times. Grieving is damn hard work but have faith you can get through it. Realise you are doing the best you can during possibly the worst time of your life and offer yourself what you would offer a friend. Kindness and compassion and do what works for you.

4. **Recognise you DO have a choice.**

You cannot control the events that happen in your life but you can choose whether you want to respond from the victim point of view or choose to have some power over your response. Do not feel helpless but rather help yourself. Recognise you are responsible for your life. As Victor Frankl wrote in *Man's Search for Meaning*, the ultimate freedom is the ability to "choose one's attitude in a given set of circumstances."

5. **'Self-Pity is a dead-end road' – Cheryl Strayed.**

Feeling sorry for yourself for a short time is normal and can provide comfort. However, left unchecked it will keep you stuck in your grief and prevent you moving forward in your healing journey. I know this to be true because I was stuck in self-pity for some time in my grief. I was angry and wanted an apology that was not forthcoming. My anger only hurt me and my family; not the people it was directed at. Those people had no idea and I assume were getting on with their lives while I was stuck.

6. Anger is a poisoned chalice. Forgiveness will bring you inner peace but the path to forgiveness is not easy.

You harm yourself holding onto anger. It will keep you stuck. Find an acceptable way to express it and move forward.

Recognise every one of us has been wronged and we have all also wronged others. Forgiving those who have hurt you will bring healing to your soul. Failing to forgive will keep you stuck in your grief journey unable to move forward.

Archbishop Desmond Tutu and his daughter, Rev Mpho Tutu have written eloquently about it in their book, *The Book of Forgiving: The Fourfold Path for Healing Ourselves and Our World*. If you are finding it challenging to forgive there is so much wisdom, guidance and support in this book.

7. Don't hide your grief from your children.

Allow children to learn it is OK to be sad and crying when missing someone important in your life whom you love. Tell them the truth about the reasons for the death/separation so they can process it and understand it. Answer their questions truthfully and appropriately for their age. Continue to do so as they grow, recognising as their intellectual capacity to comprehend increases with age they will have new questions they want answered. Teaching children to grieve effectively is a wonderful gift to them that builds their resilience to cope with life's losses.

9. Men and women seek comfort in different ways as a general rule.

In terms of intimacy in couples, grief is often dealt with so differently. Men as a general rule will seek comfort in their sexual relationship by feeling close through sexual intercourse. Whereas women tend to want cuddles and to talk to feel intimacy. There is a very high percentage of parents that separate after the death of a child. Grief will bring to the surface any unresolved issues in relationships. Bereavement doesn't make a relationship better but if people remain committed and supportive; if they can find a way to communicate their needs, they can work their way through the grief journey.

10. Reflect on the gifts in your loss.

Loss and grief can transform you. It can push you to develop new understandings of yourself; you will definitely discover strength and resilience you never imagined you had. You will have a stronger sense of self.

People often say they recognise what is truly important to them in life and change the direction of their life to a much more satisfying life. James Thomas is a great example of this. You will gain a greater understanding of how to better live your life true to yourself rather than leading a life that pleases others.

Loss can improve the way you relate to others, wanting to be more authentic, honest and loving.

Many people also report spiritual change as they discover new values and beliefs about themselves and the world with a deeper understanding of how precious life is. Addressing your spiritual needs can provide a more meaningful life.

Richard Tedeschi and Lawrence Calhoun's research article 'Post Traumatic Growth', holds that people who endure psychological struggle following adversity often see positive growth afterward.

Practice telling the people in your life "I love you," for you have learnt they may not be around tomorrow. Being of service to others as well as the people you love is a wonderful gift to yourself.

11. Honour your loved person with a legacy.

Finding meaning and purpose in your suffering through compassion for others can help you to see the possibilities for creating change. It springs from not wanting anyone else to go through the pain of grief you have experienced. Being of service to others can create a positivity, help you heal and is very rewarding if you are ready and motivated.

12. Acceptance will set you free.

Acceptance comes from bearing witness to the plain, simple facts of the loss and understanding you will be a different person because of the loss. Once you get to that place where you have as much understanding of the circumstances as possible, you can move forward.

Accept that loss and sorrow are part of every life. Accept you cannot change the past but you can build a new future. Then step by step rebuild your life.

> **66**

*Life is never made unbearable
by circumstances,*

*but only by lack of meaning
and purpose.*

Victor Frankl

Five Golden Steps to Create Meaning from Your Loss

1. Ask yourself 'Am I ready?' and if you are, decide what it is you want to prevent others experiencing. For me I wanted future bereaved parents to receive better care than our family did. I was turning my pain into compassion for others.

2. Be inspired by the people interviewed in this book who all created a legacy. Like them, create a goal by asking yourself exactly what it is you want to do. What would make you feel your loss wasn't meaningless but that it had a purpose. Preferably, create a SMART goal. By making sure the goals you set are aligned with the five SMART criteria – The Goal needs to be Specific, Measurable, Attainable, Relevant, and Time-Specific.

3. It's good to ask friends and family for their ideas and thoughts and invite them to be a part of your passion and goal. Decide on the ACTION steps required to achieve your goal. Write them down and play with them until you all feel you have a complete list. Put your Actions into a schedule, then delegate what you can to others while you manage the overall project.

4. Research if you can involve organisations to join you in a partnership. It is always easier to have a team working on it. Ask friends and family to help you. They may be delighted to support you in a practical way, as people often feel helpless with a bereaved person.

5. Recognise your legacy and the meaning and purpose it has created in your life and feel proud. **Compassion, love and helping others is as necessary for the human spirit as food, water, exercise and shelter are for the body.**

> ## Normal does not exist in grief. It is a unique, complex and chaotic journey that can leave you exhausted and feeling broken.

Karon Coombs

Author Profile

KARON COOMBS

Registered Nurse, Educator, Documentary Maker, Energy Medicine Practitioner, Author, Speaker.

Karon Coombs is a registered nurse who specialised in palliative care and oncology. She has been a nurse educator for the past 20 years and has also spoken at many state, national and international healthcare conferences on grief and bereavement.

Her extensive knowledge in this area is both professional and personal. Karon has had to deal with the loss of one of her own three children. After her son Dashiell died, she created an award-winning documentary to educate healthcare professionals about providing better care for bereaved parents in order to improve their bereavement outcome. This documentary was subsequently bought by a distributor in the Netherlands. Karon created systemic change that continues to have a ripple effect today. She is passionate about supporting bereaved people to make their grief journey easier.

Karon is a member of the Australian College of Nursing and Nepean Therapy Dogs. Her own Moodle is a therapy dog. She facilitates workshops for the bereaved and people diagnosed with a terminal disease as well as offering one-on-one sessions. Karon has studied how art can help people to heal and incorporates it into her work.

In her spare time, she loves to dance, something she's done since she was a child. Karon believes in giving back to the community and is also a volunteer for Gateway Family Services, Community Smiles and Shared Reading New South Wales.

She has travelled extensively throughout her life, visiting New Zealand, England, Wales, Scotland, France, Switzerland, Italy, Greece, Noumea, the Isle of Pines and Vanuatu.

Karon is the author of *The Grief Journey*. She currently lives in the Blue Mountains in New South Wales, Australia, with her husband and her beloved therapy dog, Teddy.

Resources

KARON COOMBS

YOU CAN CREATE A LIFE WITH MEANING AND BE HAPPY AGAIN

Do you want to feel happier and lighter?

Are you feeling alone and like no one understands?

Are you feeling stuck in your grief journey?

Are you desperate for relief from your suffering and despair?

Do you want to find inner peace and healing?

With 35 years of professional and life experience including study in the field of loss and grief, I understand people from all walks of life and can identify where they are on their grief journey. I am adept at getting to the root of the issues you face.

I also understand where you are at, because I have been there following the death of my son. I felt all the crazy emotions of the roller coaster ride of grief too and found a way to move forward to have a meaningful and fulfilling life.

I can help you develop strategies, avoid the pitfalls and mitigate the fallout so you can feel happier and move forward in your life.

Contact me to organise a one-on-one session via zoom on your computer by phoning 61 438 593 136

Or email me at – karoncoombs1@gmail.com

Or visit the website www.thegriefjourney.com.au

to find out about workshops, seminars and other events and opportunities.

Karon Coombs

Want to have a Dynamic Speaker and Trainer for Your Next Conference?

Karon can create massive and permanent change in the lives of your participants and in the day-to-day operations of your company.

Keynote

Karon is an engaging and powerful speaker who will deliver a thought-provoking program.

Full or half day Workshops

This is a tailored program aligned to the company's outcomes and objectives which utilises exercises, activities and group experiences designed to achieve much greater awareness and personal growth. Includes handouts and learning tools.

Discuss the options with Karon by phoning 61 438 593 136

Or email at - karoncoombs1@gmail.com

"Owning our story and loving ourselves through the process is the bravest thing that we will ever do."

Brene Brown

Recommended Reading List

A Grief Observed by C.S. Lewis

Coping with Grief by Mal McKissock and Dianne McKissock

Dying to Wake Up by Dr Rajiv Parti MD

Grand Plan Shattered by Dee Scown

www.DeeScown.com.au deescown111@gmail.com

Letters from Motherless Daughters by Hope Edelman

On Father by John Birmingham

Proof of Heaven by Eben Alexander

The Book of Forgiving: The Fourfold Path for Healing Ourselves and our World. By Archbishop Desmond Tutu and his daughter, Rev Mpho Tutu

Three-and-a-half Heartbeats by Amanda Prowse

Recommended Medium

Ezio and Michelle De Angelis
https://eziodeangelis.com.au/

"It's nice to be recognized for my spiritual gifts but the entire purpose of spirit communication is to affirm the continuity of life after the physical person has ceased to be. There is no death… only a new and different kind of life. In many ways, my role as a medium is to be a spirit messenger, a bridge between two worlds."

Ezio De Angelis